How to Select a
VOCATION

WITH STATISTICAL ANALYSIS OF
THREE THOUSAND BIRTH-CHARTS
AND THIRTY VOCATIONS

By Elbert Benjamine
PRESIDENT OF "THE CHURCH OF LIGHT"

☆

HOW TO SELECT A VOCATION

TABLE OF CONTENTS

	PAGE
Astro-Physical Interaction Diagram	4
CHAPTER I—How to Gauge the Natural Aptitudes	5
CHAPTER II—How to Gauge the Fortunate Associations	23
CHAPTER III—The Influence of Conditioning & Environment	41
CHAPTER IV—Astrological Constants and Statistical Analysis of 30 Vocations	59

Architect	60	Lawyer	101
Artist	63	Machinist	104
Astrologer	66	Movie Actor	107
Athlete	69	Musician	111
Aviator	72	Nurse	114
Bookkeeper	74	Policeman	116
Chemist	77	Politician	119
Cosmetician	80	Radio Technician	122
Dancer	82	Salesman	125
Dentist	84	Stenographer	128
Doctor	88	Store Clerk	131
Draftsman	90	Teacher	134
Electrician	93	Telephone Operator	136
Engineer	96	Waiter	138
Farmer	99	Writer	140

ASTRO-PHYSICAL INTERACTION DIAGRAM

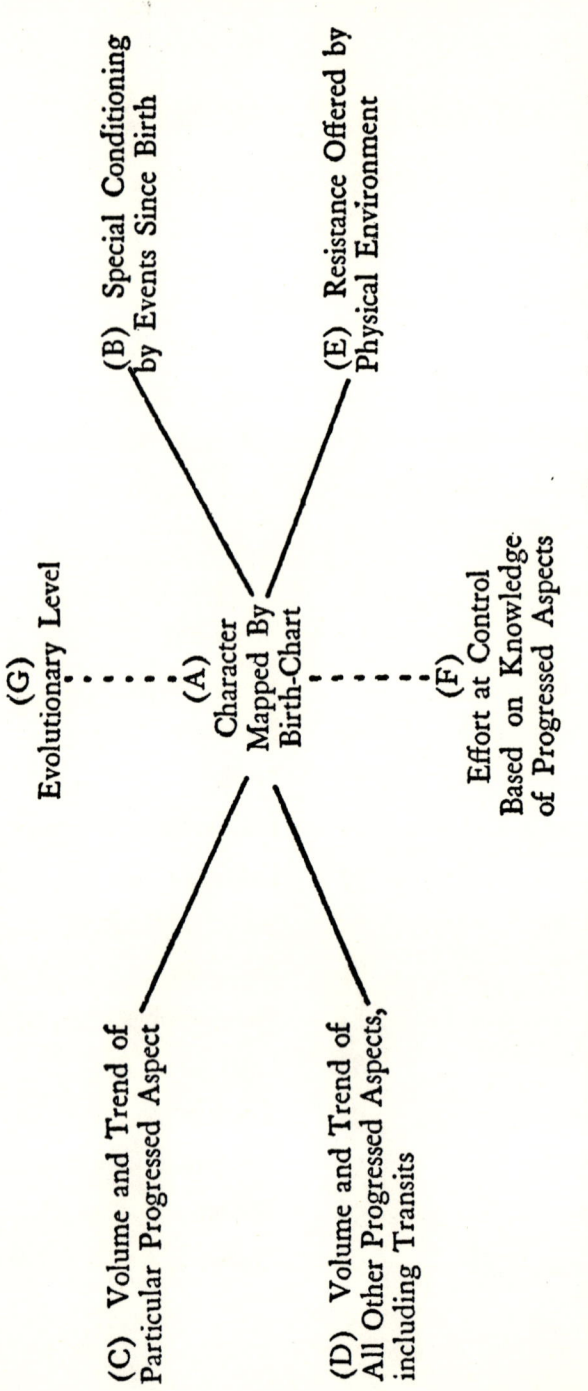

(G) Evolutionary Level

(A) Character Mapped By Birth-Chart

(B) Special Conditioning by Events Since Birth

(E) Resistance Offered by Physical Environment

(C) Volume and Trend of Particular Progressed Aspect

(D) Volume and Trend of All Other Progressed Aspects, including Transits

(F) Effort at Control Based on Knowledge of Progressed Aspects

In all problems relating to the events which come into the life — and the *practice* of a given vocation is no exception — each of the above seven factors should receive attention as playing a significant part. However, in the *selection* of a vocation (G) is of no significance, and (F) is equally significant in all vocations.

Chapter One

HOW TO GAUGE THE NATURAL APTITUDES

As this book is the outcome of 18 years continuous work by The Brotherhood of Light Astrological Research Department, to prevent possible misapprehension, it should be stated right at the start what we have endeavored to do and what we have not attempted. The Church of Light maintains three vigorous research departments to acquire more information about astrology, about extra-sensory perception, and about how to exercise control over the life, not for academic or theoretical purposes, but to be able to give people instructions of a practical nature which will help them develope the highest possibilities of their own souls, enable them to contribute their utmost to universal welfare, and thus aid in the furtherance of God's Great Evolutionary Plan.

Our interest in astrology is not to try to prove that every incident of life is predetermined by the positions of the stars. Instead, it is to find out to what extent and in what manner, astrological forces influence life—be it much or be it little—to the end of learning how these forces can best be utilized, diverted, or otherwise handled to attain the ends just set forth. How much or how little astrological energies actually influence human conduct and the events which are attracted into human lives has already been determined by the laws of Nature; and instead of trying to prove some preconception about how much life is thus influenced, or in what manner, our interest lies in finding out and utilizing the facts.

On the one hand we find the scholastic dictators who, because they cannot explain that influence, proclaim that the planets cannot have any influence over human life. On the other hand we have astrological zealots who, carried away by enthusiasm, must account for every trivial action and every inconsequential event of their lives, by either a progressed aspect or a transit. These ignore the possibility that the individual ever does anything due to his own character, or that anything ever comes into his life as the result of the inner-plane activity of his own character, except as planetary aspects releasing energy at the time influence him. They imply that man is an automaton which never makes the slightest gesture except at the instigation of an appropriate planetary aspect.

In so doing they ignore not only the individual's ability to act without some planetary prompting at the time, but also that the physical environment has a power to modify both behavior and the events attracted.

But if we consider human life as reacting not to one plane alone, but both to inner-plane forces from the planets and to the pressure of the conditions found in the physical environment, it is logical to assume that physical environment may be more powerful in its influence over the individual at some particular time than weak astrological energies which then are operative. But whether logical or not, our extensive case history studies of the events and conditions in the lives of people with almost identical birth-charts when the same progressed aspect formed in their charts prove conclusively that either the physical environment, or the conditioning by events that have happened in the past, does actually modify, in so far as the importance of the event, its fortune or misfortune, its specific nature, and the time when it happens, even those events indicated by powerful major progressed aspects.

A few of these case history studies were published in the ten issues of THE RISING STAR commencing with the April 7, 1940, issue. Others will be published in due time. They relate chiefly to the influence of progressed aspects in their power to attract events. But they are mentioned here because they also show what the birth-chart does and does not map. It does not map SPECIFIC events. But it does map PREDISPOSITIONS toward the types of conditions and events which will affect each of the 12 departments of the individual's life.

Now for astrology to perform the function in human affairs which it should, all the factors of real importance as affecting human life need to be retained and used. Yet not only to avoid error in judgment, but to make it possible for astrology to be used on the vast scale its value warrants, it should be kept as simple as possible and all the factors not of marked significance ignored. There is not much use considering astrological factors which have less power to influence the life than any one of a dozen things the individual encounters every day in his outer-plane environment. To give over-emphasis to the insignificant, is to place not enough emphasis on the really significant.

To decide just how much emphasis should be placed on each factor — astrological, conditioning, physical environment — requires great experience and delicate weighing. And to decide just where precision ends careless work, and needless time-consuming hair-splitting begins, requires keen discrimination. No doubt some difference of opinion will be held in each of these matters, due to variations both in temperament and experience; but to find out these matters is one of the jobs of The Brotherhood of Light Astrological Research Department.

Our ideal is not to present to the public something so difficult and complex that only a few individuals can master it; and not to present to the public something that is simple, but so unreliable as to be worthless. It is to be able to present to the public something which sets forth all the factors—astrological, conditioning, physical environment—in their correct relation of importance to each other, and in such a manner that any person of ordinary intelligence can, by a moderate amount of study, use it in his own life to become happier, more successful and more spiritual by far than he could have been without using it.

We want to see astrology as universally used as is the simple arithmetic by which the housewife pays her grocery bill. And for her to use astrology to benefit her life should take less effort than she used in school to acquire the knowledge of simple arithmetic which now she could ill do without.

The Brotherhood of Light Astrological Research Department began in April 1924 to solicit from as many persons as it could reach, the birth-data, including the hour of birth, of people following the various vocations, and the birth-data, including hour of birth and date the event happened, of people who had experienced some particular disease or event. We should have liked to have had a thousand or more charts of each, but after a few years in which we strained our financial resources sending out questionnaire blanks to be filled in, we became convinced that without resources far beyond our reach, it would be impossible to count on getting more than 100 timed birth-charts of each. In 18 years during which we have spent many hundred dollars each year for that purpose, we have been able to collect 100 timed birth-data each of those who follow only the 30 different vocations considered in this volume.

In the endeavor to ascertain the constant astrological factors for each vocation we were faced with two problems; the problem of acquiring the timed birth-data of those following each vocation, and the problem of locating the constant, and therefore significant, factors in the erected charts of those following each vocation. Not because we desired to limit ourselves to 100 charts of each, but because we found it beyond our ability to obtain them, we came to use 100 timed birth-charts as the basis of all our statistical work. In some of the vocations we have eventually obtained many more data and erected the charts. But in no case have we found such additional charts materially to alter the values already found in the analysis of the original 100. And as the result of the experience not merely of ourselves, but of numerous other Church of Light astrological students, we have full confidence that the values will be very much the same as those here given for each vocation irrespective of the number of additional timed birth-charts used.

During the first few years of our research work we tried out innumerable methods of tabulating the factors of the birth-chart. In fact, we exhausted our ingenuity in the endeavor to find a suitable method of applying the statistical method to astrology. What we were searching for were the constant, and therefore significant, astrological factors. From these constants to be found through statistical analysis of timed birth-charts and progressed aspects The Brotherhood of Light contemplated, and The Church of Light still contemplates, compiling a ready reference series which should include reports on all vocations, all events and conditions, and all diseases, which have a significance in human life.

The first few years of work convinced us that the signs occupied by the planets were not the constants we sought. We early found, instead, that the prominence of certain planets, and later that the activity of certain houses of the birth-chart, were usually the constant factors. Occasionally an aspect between two planets stands out. And in the analysis of charts, we have not sought to confine our attention to the prominence of planets and the activity of houses. We have invariably tabulated the signs occupied by Sun, Moon and Ascendant, and if these were of any significance have mentioned them. Likewise we have tried to discover aspects between specific planets, or any other factors that seem rather constant. And when we have found them we have tabulated and made mention of them.

It took us five years to become satisfied we could discover no better method of tabulating the birth-chart and progressed factors than the one we have since used. When we felt thus satisfied we worked up and published our first report. It was published June 1, 1929, and since that date we have been able to publish in The Church of Light Quarterly, one new report each three months, based on the analysis of 100 birth-charts.

Lenora Conwell has erected all the 5,800 birth-charts so far used in these reports, which cover the 30 vocations analyzed in this book, the 20 different events analyzed in WHEN AND

WHAT EVENTS WILL HAPPEN, and the 7 different diseases and Length of Life so far analyzed in preparing the book, BODY DISEASE AND ITS STELLAR TREATMENT. The report on Length of Life did not require progressed aspects to be calculated. But in each of the 2,700 charts relating to the time when a given event took place or a given disease developed, Lenora Conwell calculated and placed around the outside of the erected birthchart, the progressed places of the planets, M.C. and Asc. for the date of illness or other event. Both the chart work and the tabulation in reference to the 3,000 charts used as a basis for the material in this book were done by Lenora Conwell.

What These Statistical Analyses Do Not Attempt to Do—In addition to the statistical work with charts we had then been doing for 14 years, early in 1938, because of unfair and unwarranted attacks on astrology by a certain group of orthodox scientists who seek to become the dictators of the intellectual life of America, we commenced work having for its object the finding of a mathematical method through the application of which the tenets of astrology could be proved or disproved in a manner rigorous enough to satisfy even those who, because they have been emotionally conditioned against it by their schooling and their desire for significance, are prejudiced against astrology.

Such a method, to prove anything after the rigorous manner desired, must rest upon first finding the probability that the astrological condition investigated is present through chance. For instance, in the ESP work of Dr. Rhine, as there are 5 cards marked with each of the 5 symbols in the pack of 25 cards, the chances are one in five that a certain one of these symbols will appear by chance when a card is turned. But in a birth-chart the factors are tremendously more complex. The movements of the planets are not uniform. Sometimes they move faster and sometimes slower, sometimes direct in motion, sometimes retrograde. The number of aspects formed within a given period of time is variable. And in addition to aspects, the house position is of equal importance in giving prominence.

Aspects are more powerful when close than when more distant, being most powerful when the aspect is perfect. The degree of prominence is not the same in different houses, and in any house the planets exert their influence more powerfully the nearer they are to the cusp of the house. Thus are the degrees of influence so variable that, although they can be appraised through inspection well enough for practical purposes, in which refinement of weighing influences is not required, they present a complexity that makes the accurate determination of the chance probability that a certain astrological condition is present not possible by any method we have thus far been able to find, or that to date has been presented by the astronomer mathematicians.

At the time we undertook this investigation we had among our active membership several young men of outstanding mathematical ability who were willing to devote themselves to the solution of this problem. They started immediately to work, and at our annual convention on November 10, 1938, became formally The Committee to Formulate Mathematical Methods to Be Used in Statistical Studies of Astrology. These young men made themselves familiar with probability mathematics, including the latest published in mathematical journals. When J. A. Hynek, Assistant Astronomer at Perkins Observatory, wrote us December 15, 1938, of his plan to tabulate the 22,000 names in the American Men of Science, list the aspects of Mercury and apply Poisson's Law, they gave it as their opinion that such procedure would prove absolutely nothing. In the first place, they pointed out, Poisson's Law, except for special problems, was in discredit by up-to-date mathematicians, and in the second place it could not with validity be applied to this problem.

We had decided, cost what it might in labor, to do whatever tabulating and mathematical work might be necessary to test out certain astrological tenets, providing an unassailable formula could be found. The amount of work these young men put in on this problem was stupendous. But in spite of that effort they did not produce a formula which they felt would stand up, and truly prove or disprove any of the outstanding astrological tenets, against the anticipated attacks of professional mathematicians.

They pointed out that with such a simple problem as the probability that a certain symbol of Dr. Rhine's ESP cards would be drawn—where there were only 5 characters, and each of these present only 5 times in a pack of 25—there has been a squabble lasting half a dozen years as to the validity of the probability mathematics employed; and that finally, to determine whether the probability mathematics were or were not sound, an actual run of half a million chance selections were made and recorded at Duke University. If in such a simple matter the mathematicians failed to agree, they felt there was small hope they would agree on the validity of any formula they had found, in a matter where prejudice was equally great, and the complexity of possible factors involved was tremendous.

I relate these facts here for two purposes: One is to point out that our tables based on the statistical analysis of birth-charts and progressed aspects, while suitable as a basis for astrological judgment, were not compiled, nor are they suitable, for the purpose of proving the validity of astrology. While we had hoped to compile tables by which such validity could be tested, after four arduous years, due to the demands of the war on the members of our mathematical committee, this effort has now been abandoned for the duration of the world conflict. The other point is that, up to the present time, no statistical work has been done which disproves the validity of astrology.

Those interested in discrediting astrology point to the studies of Farnsworth and Hynek. Dr. Farnsworth had found it stated in certain astrological books that persons born under Libra should have musical ability. But looking up the birth-dates of 1,498 musicians, he found that fewer were born under this sign than any other except Scorpio. Therefore he held astrology was wrong. These findings were published in TIME magazine, issue of May 16, 1938.

Now it is possible to take books published twenty years ago on any material science and show by the findings of scientific men since then that certain statements in these books are incorrect. We do not know what astrological books Dr. Farnsworth consulted, but certainly not any B. of L. text book; for in Brotherhood of Light Report No. 2, published September 1, 1929, the signs were tabulated in which the Sun, Moon and Ascendant were found in the birth-charts of 100 instrumental musicians. Virgo, Aquarius and Pisces were highest, Leo next highest, Taurus lowest and Capricorn next lowest. Among vocal musicians Leo was highest and Capricorn lowest. Among none was Libra a high sign; and if Sun sign alone had been tabulated it might have been lowest. This Report, reproduced in this book, had so wide a circulation that I am sure it was not generally held by astrological students after 1929 that Libra gave musical ability. Dr. Farnsworth merely set up a straw man, and then knocked it down.

As to the Hynek so-called investigation, not only did our mathematicians decide before he used them that his probability mathematics were invalid when applied to the problem as he used them—a decision since upheld by non-astrological mathematicians—but he started on the assumption that Men of Science —to which group he belongs—are the intelligent people. No doubt it does take brains such as are mapped by a prominent Mercury to make a scientist, but so does it to give the kind of brains used in a wide number of other pursuits. There are other factors which turn the mind to science, other planets also prominent no doubt, but we will not know what they are until we have the timed birth-charts of 100 men of science. As I wrote Hynek on December 21, 1938:

"As among the 19 vocations we have so far covered we have not yet analyzed 100 birth-charts of scientists. I can not say whether or not Mercury is prominent in their charts. It was thus found prominent in the charts of writers and school teachers, and strangely enough to a somewhat less degree in the charts of movie stars and telephone operators, these latter requiring an alertness of intelligence. . . .

"Until we analyze the charts of 100 scientists, I would not know if Mercury is prominent in their charts, or what other planets are prominent in their charts. We have made it a point not to speculate on such matters, but to get the 100 charts and find out from them."

Thus not only is the mathematical method used by Hynek unreliable, but he has assumed that Mercury is the special planet of scientists, and having set up a straw man, has used his unreliable mathematical method to knock it down.

I am pointing out that so far no valid mathematical formula has been used in any real test of astrology, because the assumption that it has may deliver a blow to true astrological investigation, as faulty mathematics thus retarded for many years the investigation of extra-sensory perception.

In 1917 Professor John E. Coover of Stanford University published a 600-page volume reporting the conclusion that thought transference was not present in the many subjects he tested. Because of the size, detail, and apparent exhaustiveness of his work, and that it was done in a university of good standing, it was regarded as an authoritative scientific treatment of the subject. Professor Coover used an elaborate statistical evalution of his results that gave an impression of finality. As a result the impression in university circles was that telepathy had been exploded and there was no use investigating it further. And this attitude persisted until Dr. Rhine published his experiments at Duke University many years later.

Dr. Edward B. Tichener, of Cornell University, many years ago also wrote a paper which discouraged investigation along this line. He reported tests carried out to ascertain if people could tell reliably when they were being stared at from behind. He concluded not. Also that there was nothing to telepathy. Dr.

Tichener was a well-known psychologist, but unfamiliar with the methods for statistical evaluation. One of his graduates reports that on a certain occasion a percipient called almost entirely correctly down through a pack of playing cards, naming both suit and rank. Yet Professor Tichener was disappointed because the percipient failed to name every one of the 52 cards correctly. He held that if thought transference were a reality the percipient should be able to get a perfect score.

Such reports from university professors as those of Coover and Tichener for many years blocked further investigation of telepathy. It created a prejudice which exists even now after a great many other university professors have demonstrated telepathy to be a fact. It almost enabled the materialists completely to suppress such investigation. Yet at least five persons familiar with probability mathematics and duly qualified for such work have, in view of present-day findings, gone over the statistics of Professor Coover's experiments in thought transference, and they are unanimous in the conclusion that Coover was mistaken, and in fact his experiments can not be explained by chance alone, but are in reality outstanding evidence of thought transference.

Unintentionally Professor Coover, Dr. Tichener, and some other investigators whose names carried weight, almost placed the investigation of what is now called ESP permanently in its grave. And I call attention to the fact that so far there has been no valid mathematical formula used in any real test of astrology, so that the danger will be lessened that other well-meaning persons, and some who are not so well-meaning, will not through similar faulty procedure lay astrology permanently to rest in the opinion of academic minds.

Our Attempts to Refine the Method Used—The chief factor in determining the natural aptitude for a given vocation is the relative prominence of the various planets in the timed chart of birth. And for 14 years we had been judging this relative prominence by inspecting the chart and applying certain general rules which will be explained later. But in 1938 we set our group of mathematical young men to work on the problem of finding formulas by which the personal equation of the astrologer should be eliminated, and the volume of energy mapped by each planet in a chart should be determined with precision in relation to the volume of energy mapped by each of the other planets in the same chart. Also we set them to work on the problem of finding mathematical formulas which should determine with similar precision the relative harmony or discord of the planets in a chart due to the aspects they receive. This so-called Luck factor is the other important element in selecting a vocation. Furthermore, we sent out a call to our teachers in various places to help solve these two problems.

Will P. Benjamine and Lawrence R. Dunsmoor put much work into finding the mathematical method desired, and some of their conclusions were published in the December, 1938, and January and February, 1939, issues of THE RISING STAR. A definite mathemtaical formula for determining prominence to be expressed in star-force units, called Astro-Dynes, was presented. And in the June, 1939, issue, a formula was published for determining the harmony of a planet.

With no knowledge of the work done by W. P. Benjamine and Dunsmoor, very similar formulas for determining prominence and harmony of planets were worked out by Mrs. H. S. D. Starnaman and Mr. Honsberger of Toronto, Canada, and mailed to us on February 13, 1939. Attempts to solve these problems were also made and submitted by a number of other students.

These systems of determining precise prominence must of necessity start from assumptions based upon experience that certain house areas represent definite volumes of energy in relation to various other house areas in the chart, that each aspect represents definite volumes of energy in relation to the other nine possible aspects, and that within the orb of its operation each degree the aspect is distant from perfect diminishes the energy it maps by a specified amount. And when all these different factors are dealt with in the detail necessary to secure precision the amount of work required to handle them quite precludes their being used in the statistical analysis of series each of which include 100 charts. Furthermore, the detailed labor and mathematics involved also precludes their being used by the ordinary astrological student.

Both for the sake of the statistician doing research work, and for the sake of the ordinary astrological student who wishes to apply the findings of the statistician to the charts of those who consult him, to be of practical value, the method of prominence determination and harmony determination must be not only as precise as possible, but quickly and easily applied.

But before indicating the method of chart inspection which we have used in all the statistical work done by us to date, and which, because up to the present time we have found more satisfactory, we continue to use, the real source of natural aptitudes should be explained.

The Real Source of Any Natural Aptitude—Astrological energies have an influence over human life because man and every other physical thing exist both on the outer plane and the inner plane. The inner-plane organization is the pattern which the physical form tends to fill in, and does so to the extent physical materials and the outer-plane environment permit. It is common to express this thought by saying that every physical object has an astral counterpart. But in the case of man, the inner-plane organization may also embrace energies finer than the astral, called spiritual. Substance that attains a velocity greater than that of light is no longer either physical or electromagnetic, but inner-plane. If the velocities exceed that of astral substance, the conditions and properties exist which are those of the spiritual plane.

Man has a physical body composed of substance which has the velocities which we associate with matter. Interpenetrating this physical form is the electromagnetic body composed of Boundary-Line energies, such as have approximately the velocity of light and other electromagnetic phenomena. And interpenetrating both of these lower-velocity forms is the astral body, whose substance has velocities in excess of those of light. The inner-plane body can affect the physical body, and the physical can affect the inner-plane body, only through the Boundary-Line energies which contact both outer-plane and inner-plane substances.

The inner-plane organization of man is identical with what the psychologists call the unconscious mind. What is generally referred to as the subconscious mind partakes in varying degrees of Boundary-Line organization. But what the psychologists call the unconscious mind is identical with the soul.

The inner-plane form has been built of inner-plane substance by states of consciousness. If we use the term thought to embrace feeling, emotion, and perception as well as the cerebral processes of man, we are correct in saying the inner-plane body of man is entirely built by thought. It has, in fact, been organized by all the states of consciousness which the soul has experienced in its evolution. The soul has evolved through many lower forms of life, from mineral up to man; and its various experiences have, through the states of consciousness accompanying them, organized progressively a more complex inner-plane form. When the soul is born into the human form, its inner-plane body has within its organization the sum total of those past experiences in lower forms, those from the astral regions between successive incarnations where assimilation and reorganization occur, those derived from contact with the hereditary germ-cells of its physical parents, and those acquired through the mother during the period of gestation.

Astral substance which has been organized by states of consciousness forms the basic psychoplasm of the finer form, even as the physical body is composed of protoplasm and its secretions. But all protoplasm is not the same, and all psychoplasm is not the same. The chemical composition on the one hand, and the thought composition on the other, vary. Also, as the body is composed of cells of protoplasm organized into definite structures, so is the psychoplasm composed of thought-elements of different kinds, organized in the finer form into thought-cells and thought structures. Because these partake of planetary qualities, and are mapped by the planets, they are also called stellar-cells and stellar structures.

The planets in their movements through the heavens form definite patterns with their interlocking fields of force. The soul of an individual before birth also has a pattern composed of thought-cells and thought structures definitely organized by its past experiences. If the thought-cell pattern which is the real character of the individual is widely different than the pattern of astrological force present at the time of its physical birth, the child does not live. The rule is, however, that when the two patterns closely coincide it is easy for the child to be born, and most children are born when the two patterns do rather closely coincide.

It should be repeatedly emphasized that what the planets map in the birth-chart are not events or conditions of life, but states of consciousness which have been organized as the thought-cells and thought structures of the soul by experiences in life-forms lower in the scale of evolution than the human. The positions of the planets at birth do not cause the individual then born to possess the characteristics they indicate. Instead, the positions of the planets at any given time indicate the direction in which their energies are flowing and combining with other planetary currents. And the sum total of these energy streams and their convergences form an inner-plane energy pattern.

Now a pattern of steel is quite rigid, and anything of size to pass through its apertures must rigidly conform in outline to them. A similar pattern of rubber is more elastic. A glove of rather heavy rubber, for instance, may be made to conform to average size hands which vary rather widely in detail, even if not elastic enough to permit entry of a large hand, or to fit a small hand. Nor will such a glove adapt itself to the foot or head. Likewise a pattern of swiftly flowing water, as from the perforations in a nozzle, can be deflected within limits without splashing and spoiling the general design.

The exact amount of rigidity and the limit of elasticity afforded by an astrological pattern as an opportunity for a soul to be born into human form remains yet to be determined. Yet actual observation of people born with almost identical birth-charts indicates considerable elasticity does exist. It seems that, when proper physical conditions also are present, souls can be born in human form who correspond in the broader features of their thought-cell organization to the planetary pattern, but who vary considerably from it in detail.

Now experiences, whether of lower life-forms or of man, naturally fall into ten different categories, each category being of a type which gives it the same general quality as that of one of the ten planets. The more experience a soul has had, or the more intense it is, of a given planetary type, the greater amount of the corresponding thought-element is built into the structure of the soul, and the more energy the thought-cells thus possess. And thought-cell activity is the real source of any natural aptitude.

The planets of a birth-chart, by their prominence, map the degree of thought-cell activity of each of the ten different thought-element families. Where the planet is actually located maps the group of thought-cells belonging to this planetary family which are most active, and have been organized into a dynamic stellar structure. The houses which a planet rules through the signs on their cusps, but which it does not occupy, map the less active common thought-cells belonging to the same planetary family.

Thus does the prominence of a planet in a birth-chart measure the thought-cell activity of one definite kind. And this thought-cell activity not only indicates the volume and intensity of the experiences of that type which formed the thought-cells, but also the natural aptitude for expressing ability of a corresponding sort.

It should be remembered, however, that the natural aptitudes at birth have as yet been given no special vocational trends. They are the raw thought-cell energies of definite volumes and types which can be diverted into any channels not inconsistent with their nature, but they are not developed abilities. They must be conditioned, educated by experience or training, to flow into such special channels.

Even as in human life, the soul while animating lower life-forms, has had experiences which in many respects were not identical. These experiences have been of the Mars type, the Saturn type, or of some other planetary type, and they have been brought together in certain intensities of harmony or discord, as shown by the birth-chart aspects, and relate more pronouncedly to definite departments of life, as indicated by the houses the planets rule. But they have not been human experiences. They have not been experiences in bookkeeping, in finances, in trading, in conventional relations, in driving automobiles, in cooking, in studying books, in writing, lecturing or science.

The Mars experiences may have been such that given a proper human environment they easily are developed to give mechanical ability, or ability as a surgeon or soldier. The Saturn experiences may be such that given a proper human environment, they readily give aptitude in organizing and buying. The Jupiter experiences may have been such that given a proper human environment they develop salesmanship ability. But until conditioned by physical environment they remain merely natural aptitudes and not abilities ready for exercise.

Measuring the Natural Aptitudes—Every aspect a planet makes in a birth-chart indicates a stellar aerial stretching across the astral body and picking up planetary energy of the types indicated by its terminals and adding it to the thought-cells of the soul. The more powerful the aspect, the more energy it picks up, and the more activity given to the thought-cells mapped by the planets which form its terminals. Thus do aspects reveal thought-cell activity.

As the Sun rules electrical energies and the Moon the magnetic energies which together comprise the electromagnetic form, the planetary energies of the Sun and those of the Moon have direct access to this boundary-line body. And as the planet Mercury rules the nerves and the electric currents which flow over them in response to thought, its planetary energies also have direct access to the electromagnetic body. Now the energies of the soul which reach and have an influence upon the physical body, must use electromagnetic energies as a conductor. And as any other planet in aspect to the Sun, Moon or Mercury thus also has direct access to electromagnetic energies, it is able to make its influence felt more markedly in the physical world than if its stellar aerial did not thus connect up with these electromagnetic energies.

Yet even aside from its aspects, any planet in an angle indicates that its energies in reaching the finer body and the thought-cells it maps, meet little resistance, and that therefore, more of its energies reach and influence the individual than were it not so located.

When a planet receives very powerful aspects, especially if a heavy aspect is not more than one degree from perfect, it must be considered prominent irrespective of not being in an angle and aspecting Sun, Moon or Mercury. But such prominence constitutes an exception to the general rule that only such planets in a birth-chart as are in an angle, or which aspect Sun, Moon or Mercury with a reasonable degree of closeness, are to be considered prominent. Determining the relative degree of prominence of a planet is important, because the amount of its prominence is the measure of the thought-cell activity of the type the planet maps.

In astrology, even more than in most sciences, because it deals with that very complex whole known as the human character, there are exceptions to nearly all general rules. That which usually indicates one thing, may not indicate it in special cases where some other set of factors is present which pulls strongly in a different direction.

Because any mechanical method so far advanced for the precise determination of the relative prominence of each planet in a chart of birth rests solely on assumptions derived from observation, and is too cumbersome for general use, all the analyses of the 3,000 timed birth-charts presented in this book have considered planets prominent when in angles and when in reasonably close aspect to Sun, Moon or Mercury, with only an occasional planet considered prominent otherwise because its aspects were too powerful to be ignored, or because in addition to weakly aspecting Sun, Moon or Mercury it was also powerfully aspected otherwise.

The analysis of 100 birth-charts of people who follow a given occupation, and whose hour of birth is known, reveals that certain planets are almost invariably prominent in all these charts. They may be considered the birth-chart constants of those occupations.

We may be confident, therefore, that any other person who has the same birth-chart constants, has the groundwork for similar abilities, and an aptitude for the given kind of work. We may even go further, and feel sure that the natural aptitude of any person for a given pursuit, relative to his other aptitudes, can accurately be measured by the prominence of the birth-chart constants of that vocation in his birth-chart. That is, the greater the activity of the thought-cells which statistical analysis has revealed to be the most essential in following the occupation, the more aptitude for that occupation the individual possesses.

We have published the birth-data of many of the series of 100 charts used, and when the facilities are present will finish publishing the balance of the 3,000. It may be that those using other methods of determining prominence, or who have a different personal equation in using this one, in analyzing these charts will get quite different percentages. But we are confident that if they use any valid method of determining prominence, they will find the same planets prominent for each vocation as those here given. Therefore the student who has a little experience, and can gauge even roughly the relative prominence of the planets in any chart, also from the analyses here presented will be able to determine the relative degree of natural aptitudes of an individual for following each of the different vocations.

What we have attempted to do in applying the statistical method to these birth-charts, is to use the ordinary method of inspection astrologers everywhere employ to gauge the influences in a birth-chart, and to present findings based on methods already familiar to almost all astrologers; which will enable them, or any astrological student who has learned to judge a birth-chart, readily to determine the best vocation an individual can follow. We have striven for practical results, and the letters which have been coming in over many years from astrologers and astrological students lead us to believe in this we have been successful.

Harmony or Discord of a Planet Has Little Significance Relative to Ability—There is a decided difference between having ability of a certain kind and good fortune in its use. The aptitude for using energy of a certain type depends primarily upon experiences in the past in using that type of energy. The natural aptitude for the use of each of the ten types of energy, as shown by the birth-chart, depends upon the pre-human experiences in using those kinds of energy; and the amount of such experience, and the activity of the thought-cells resulting from such experience, are mapped in the chart of birth by the prominence of the planets whose energies are of the same type as those experiences.

One who has followed the analyses of the large number of birth-charts of outstanding people published in the various astrological magazines by The Church of Light, from this alone will have become convinced that an afflicted planet indicates quite as much ability of its kind as a planet well aspected.

As a regular part of the class-work each week since 1915, the students of The Brotherhood of Light lessons in Los Angeles have been analyzing the birth-charts of prominent people. And this work has demonstrated quite conclusively that a heavily afflicted planet indicates outstanding ability of its kind quite as often as does a more harmonious planet.

In other words, it is the AMOUNT AND INTENSITY of the experiences of a definite type which have accumulated in the thought-cells of the soul, rather than the harmony or discord of those experiences, which determine the natural aptitude for a particular kind of work. Therefore to the extent the relative degree of activity of each group of thought-cells mapped by the ten planets can be precisely determined, to the same degree of precision can be determined the amount of natural aptitude of each of the ten types relative to the same individual's other natural aptitudes. But for reasons later to be explained this gives only the degree in which the aptitudes are present relative to each other, and not necessarily the degree of aptitude which the individual possesses in comparison to some other individual.

House Activity Has Aptitude Significance—Experiences in lower forms of life have been associated with the various departments of life in varying degree. That is, they have been experiences in mating, ruled by the seventh house, in home building, ruled by the fourth house, in short journeys, ruled by the third house, in acquisition, ruled by the second house, with the offspring, ruled by the fifth house, etc. In fact, every experience belongs to one of the twelve departments of life the thought-cells pertaining to which are mapped by the twelve houses of the birth-chart.

As distinct from the dynamic stellar structure mapped by the actual position of a planet in the birth-chart, the less vigorous and less well organized thought-cells mapped by a house of the birth-chart are called common thought-cells. The volume of activity they possess, and therefore their ability to direct the behavior and the thoughts into channels related to the department of life mapped by the house, and their ability to attract events relative to this department of life, are shown by the prominence of the planet ruling the house-cusp.

While a planet actually in a house represents thought-cells more active than those of the vacant house whose cusp it rules, a planet actually in a house, but having a few and weak aspects, may not map thought-cells as active as the common thought-cells of some vacant house whose planetary ruler is powerful by position and makes powerful aspects. Thus in judging the thought-cell activity of a given house, not only the aspects of any planet in the house must be considered, but also the aspects and prominence of the planet ruling the cusp of the house; for it maps the volume of activity of the common thought-cells.

If the thought-cells mapped by the second house are not active, the individual has not been conditioned by pre-human experiences to attract many important human events in which money is involved. If the thought-cells mapped by the sixth house (illness) and the twelfth house (hospitals and confinement) are not quite active it is unlikely the individual will make a good doctor or a good nurse, because he has little power to attract events and conditions with which a nurse or doctor must constantly associate. If the thought-cells mapped by the third house are weak, he will find accountancy a bore; for it takes active third-house thought-cells to make a person enjoy long hours writing down figures in a book. To attract one to the land as a successful farmer should be attracted, the fourth-house thought-cells should be active. And as a final illustration, no matter how much dramatic talent an individual has, unless he also has active fifth-house thought-cells he is unlikely to attract stage or screen experiences often enough to excel as an actor.

Chapter Two

HOW TO GAUGE THE FORTUNATE ASSOCIATIONS

Both his behavior and the events which come into any individual's life are the result of the thought-cell activity of his soul, or unconscious mind, acting upon and reacting from his environment. And it is because a birth-chart and progressed aspects give so good a picture of the thought-cell activity at birth, and at given periods in the life, that they can be used to determine the best vocation and the type of events that probably will occur during certain intervals of time.

The thought-cell activity primarily is derived from experiences of the type indicated by the planet mapping it; but may be greatly accentuated by planetary energy when the planet mapping it forms a progressed aspect. That is, experiences of a given type both before birth and after birth, and the planetary energies of this type released by progressed aspects, increase the thought-cell activity of this type through giving these thought-cells added energy with which to work from the inner plane to influence the objective thinking and to exert pressure on external environment to bring about events characteristic of their type. And it is the volume of thought-cell activity of a given type which determines the natural aptitude for physical activities of this type.

Yet both experiences and planetary forces when added to the thought-cells do something more than increase the thought-cell activity. They give the thought-cells—which have independent intelligence and independence of action comparable to, yet greater than, those of the cells of the physical body—harmonious or discordant desires. To the extent the experiences or the planetary energies received by the thought-cells are pleasurable do these thought-cells have desires in harmony with those of the individual in whose soul they reside, and therefore work to bring into his life the things he desires. But to the extent the experiences or the planetary energies received by the thought-cells are painful do these thought-cells have desires discordant to those of the individual in whose soul they reside, and therefore work to bring into his life events and conditions the reverse of those he desires.

This is the reason harmonious progressed aspects tend to influence the behavior favorably and tend to coincide with fortunate events, and that discordant progressed aspects tend to influence the behavior unfavorably and tend to coincide with unfortunate events. But the fortune or the misfortune of the events which come into the life are not solely dependent upon the harmony or discord of the thought-cell activity. To a great extent, often to an equal extent, they are also dependent upon the facilities of the outer-plane environment to provide events and conditions such as the active thought-cells work to attract.

While there seems no way of testing this idea statistically, the analysis of 3,000 timed birth-charts in connection with the vocation followed—some being of those who have met with marked success and some being of those who have succumbed to difficulties or disaster—leaves the impression that on an average ability and so-called luck are about equally important in making a success of any given vocation. If the individual has sufficient natural aptitude, as indicated by the constants for the vocation being exceptionally prominent, he may be successful in spite of tremendous obstacles encountered. Or if the individual is lucky enough, as indicated by harmoniously aspected planets, he may have some success even though the constants of the vocation are not very prominent. But usually, for pronounced success, the constants of the vocation must be outstandingly prominent, even though all afflicted, and there must be at least one powerful harmonious aspect where his environmental associations are concerned, insuring that at least occasionally he will have so-called luck working with him instead of always against him.

It should be apparent that no individual, however lucky he may be, can exercise abilities he does not possess. On the other hand, no matter how great the abilities of an individual are in reference to a certain occupation, if he employs these abilities amid environmental associations sufficiently discordant, disaster will overtake him.

A powerful and well aspected planet in the birth-chart indicates the environmental associations which, in the exercise of whatever talents the individual possesses, tend to attract to him so-called good luck. The good luck is attracted because the environment affords just those factors that the harmonious thought-cells mapped by the planet most readily can manipulate. As these thought-cells are active and powerful, and their desires coincide with the desires of the individual, not only are they able to influence the thinking and behavior, and working from the inner plane bring external events to pass, but the behavior and the events thus experienced are of a nature favorable to the individual.

In many vocations there is a wide variety of environmental

associations in which it is possible to exercise the special talents. A salesman, for instance, might sell munitions of war, or he might sell imported silk; and the fortune attracted in the first instance be as good or as bad as Mars in his birth-chart; or in the second instance, in which silk was sold, be as good or as bad as his birth-chart Venus.

Although in both instances a salesman, he might be blown to bits in the Mars association, provided Mars were sufficiently afflicted, because his environmental associations would give unusual opportunity for the Mars thought-cells to bring about the discordant things they desire; and he might accumulate ease and a fortune selling silk, if Venus were sufficiently powerful and harmonious, because his environmental associations would offer great resistance to the events the Mars thought-cells would desire to bring about, and ample facilities for the harmonious events the Venus thought-cells would desire and work to bring to pass. Yet neither Venus nor Mars is a birth-chart constant of salesmen.

As another example, we might consider a lawyer, exceedingly clever, using his talents to free underworld characters from impending justice. If Pluto, ruling the underworld, were sufficiently discordant, the lawyer might very well become a victim of gang warfare, because the thought-cells mapped by Pluto would desire and work for events which would be disastrous to him. Yet the same lawyer, avoiding the Pluto associations, might become opulent through working with matters ruled by the best planet in his chart; working for wealthy business men, for instance, if Jupiter were prominent and well aspected in his birth-chart.

In addition to affording the facilities with which the thought-cells mapped by the planet ruling the environmental associations can bring into the life events which are as fortunate or unfortunate as the thought-cells are harmonious or discordant, all things radiate an energy of the type of the sign or planet ruling them which is similar in its effect upon the thought-cells, although usually weaker in power, to the energy of the sign or planet. These character vibrations of the things closely associated with, as well as the individual's thoughts and astrological energies, thus impart energy to the thought-cells of similar astrological rulership and increase their activity. Because the thought-cells having the same vibrations as the close environmental associations become more active, they do more work. And the events attracted due to the increased work they are able to do is as fortunate or unfortunate as their harmony or discord.

For two reasons, therefore—additional thought-cell activity, and facilities for producing events—the individual will have better luck if he associates with the things ruled by well-aspected planets than if he associates with things ruled by discordantly aspected planets. In fact—although ability may be more than sufficient to counteract bad luck—the extent of the luck, good or bad, amid specific environmental associations is broadly indicated by the aspects of the planet ruling these associations. Broadly indicated only; because experiences since birth may have conditioned the thought-cells mapped by the planet to be either more discordant or more harmonious than they were at birth.

As the environmental associations thus importantly affect the so-called luck of every person according to aspects in his chart of birth, a list of those ruled by each of the ten planets may be made of much practical value:

SUN: gold, the government, politics, persons of authority, persons of the male sex, employers.

MOON: silver, liquids, the common people, commodities, hotels, the home, food, the female sex, rhythmic music.

MERCURY: books railroads, vehicles of travel, periodicals, telephone, telegraph, agents, people who are literary or studious.

VENUS: flowers, artistic objects, dancing, wearing apparel, fancy goods, confectionary, pastry, toilet articles, jewelry, harmonious music, people of a social turn.

MARS: war, soldiers, surgeons, mechanics, cooks, machinery, steel, implements of construction or destruction, intoxicating drink.

JUPITER: merchandise, ships, judges, church, clergymen, bankers, professional men, persons of wealth.

SATURN: basic utilities such as minerals, hay, grain, coal and building material; mines, real estate, the land, the weather, business methods, sedate or elderly people.

· URANUS: inventions, automobiles, electricity, late mechanical devices, antiques, astrology, the occult, orators, lawyers, electricians, astrologers, psychologists.

NEPTUNE: promoters, colonies, schemes requiring incorporation or profit-sharing of a number of people, feeling extra-sensory perception, oil, gas, drugs, the drama, moving pictures, avaition, mediums, mystics, psychic people, psychic energy.

PLUTO: radio, television, chemistry, inner-plane forces, intellectual or feeling extra-sensory perception, racketeers, gangsters, the coercive thoughts of others, highly spiritual people working for the benefit of society.

The thought-cells of which the inner-plane form is composed

not only have vibratory rates of the same tone as the signs and planets, but they have been formed by experiences relating to the twelve departments of life; and the thought-cells relating to any one department of life are mapped by the house of the birth-chart governing it. Experiences in lower life-forms have been with mating, home building, journeys, acquisition, offspring, and to some extent with each of the departments of life ruled by the twelve houses of the birth-chart. The amount and intensity of the experiences relating to a given department of life determine the degree of activity of the thought-cells mapped by the birth-chart house which rules it.

In addition to the number and intensity of the experiences with a given department of life, however, the pleasure or pain accompanying these experiences also is important. Painful experiences with the mate, for instance, build discords into the thought-cells mapped by the seventh house. The discordant desires with which the seventh house thought-cells are thus conditioned—whether the experiences were before or after human birth—cause them to work to bring into the life unfortunate events relating to marriage. Happy experiences in acquisition build harmonies into the thought-cells mapped by the second house. The harmonious desires with which the second house thought-cells are thus conditioned—whether the conditioning was before human birth or after it—cause them to work from the inner plane with whatever energy they possess, or acquire from progressed aspects, to bring fortunate events into the life where money or personal possessions are concerned.

Each of the twelve departments or life might thus be mentioned in its turn, in connection with the desires imparted to the thought-cells they map by the pain or pleasure of the experiences which built them, with the object of showing how the thought-cells have been thus conditioned to attract fortunate or unfortunate events relative to that particular department of life. But the significant factor is that the planet or planets ruling a given house of the birth-chart, by its aspects, shows the kind of harmony or discord that was built into the thought-cells relative to the given department of life before birth, and therefore the kind of good fortune or misfortune for which these thought-cells will try to work. Each of the ten aspects shows the kind of events the thought-cells mapped by the aspected planet have been conditioned to work for thus:

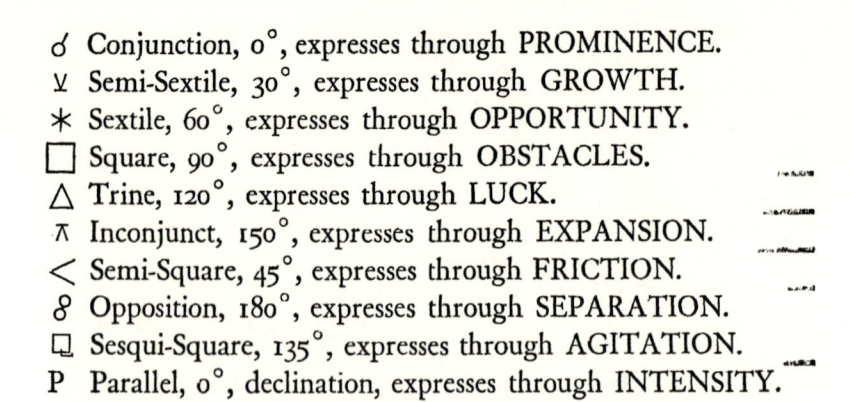

☌ Conjunction, 0°, expresses through PROMINENCE.
⚺ Semi-Sextile, 30°, expresses through GROWTH.
✶ Sextile, 60°, expresses through OPPORTUNITY.
☐ Square, 90°, expresses through OBSTACLES.
△ Trine, 120°, expresses through LUCK.
⚻ Inconjunct, 150°, expresses through EXPANSION.
∠ Semi-Square, 45°, expresses through FRICTION.
☍ Opposition, 180°, expresses through SEPARATION.
⚼ Sesqui-Square, 135°, expresses through AGITATION.
P Parallel, 0°, declination, expresses through INTENSITY.

Therefore, in general, to the extent the individual associates with a given department of life, does he give opportunity for the thought-cells mapped by the house governing this department to bring to pass the kind of events signified by the aspects to the planet or planets ruling this house. If he has a badly afflicted sixth house, for instance, not only will difficulty be attracted where whatever work he does is concerned, but if he associates much with people who are ill, as must a doctor, a nurse, or a dentist, he will encounter many difficulties of the types shown by the aspects. His sixth house associations will both increase the activity and power of the sixth-house thought-cells to attract events, and afford them environmental facilities for bringing to pass the kind of events they desire.

On the other hand, if he has a well aspected fourth house ruler, he will tend to attract good luck, not only in his own home, but through associating with lands, mines, farms, hotels, restaurants, etc., because these will add energy to his fourth-house thought-cells, giving them more power to attract events; and will afford them the environmental facilities for bringing to pass the kind of events they desire.

Here it is rather easy to make a mistake in judgment, however; for in reference to a given vocation it commonly is more important to have unusually active thought-cells relative to the department of life with which the vocation associates the individual than to have harmonious thought-cells. In other words, unless the planet ruling the house with which the individual must associate in the vocation is strongly aspected or otherwise prominent, the individual can make too little contact with the indicated department of life to make much of a success of the vocation. But if the house is active, even though badly afflicted, he may very well have ability enough to make a success of the vocation in spite of many difficulties encountered.

As one with little experience is apt to decide against a vocation because the ruler of the house indicating its close association is rather heavily afflicted, in the analysis of those vocations in which house activity is significant we have indicated not only in what percentage the house under consideration was active, but the percentage in which the house is more discordant than harmonious and the percentage in which the house is more harmonious than discordant. The difference between these two percentages indicates those in which the harmony and discord are about evenly balanced. From a scrutiny of these tables it will be seen that commonly the house with which the vocation is closely associated is more discordant than harmonious. Nevertheless, usually, in addition to powerfully discordant aspects which indicate thought-cell activity, there is also one strong harmonious aspect, or several weak harmonious aspects to its ruler.

Of the harmonious aspects the trine is most powerful, the sextile next in power, and the semi-sextile of moderate power. Of the discordant aspects the opposition is most powerful, the square next in power, and the semi-square and sesqui-square of moderate power. The conjunction has about the power of the opposition; the parallel is less well defined, being slower and diffusive; and the inconjunct has about the power of the semi-sextile. But these three aspects in themselves are neither harmonious nor discordant. They are harmonious when between harmonious planets and discordant when between discordant planets. And in calculating the aspects, the degree on the cusp of the Ascendant and the degree on the cusp of the M.C.—but not the degree on the cusp of any other houses—should be handled as if they were planets.

The aspects indicate the harmony and discord of the thought-cells mapped at birth by the houses the aspecting planets rule, and these houses in turn indicate the phases of life which the thought-cells affect thus:

FIRST HOUSE: The physical body and its health, the quality of the personal magnetism, the temperament and disposition, and purely personal changes.

SECOND HOUSE: Money and other personal possessions.

THIRD HOUSE: Brethren, private thoughts and studies, neighbors.

FOURTH HOUSE: The home, hotels, restaurants, the father,

real estate, mining, crops on the ground, and the condition at the end of life.

FIFTH HOUSE: Pleasures, love affairs, speculation, stocks and bonds, children, and entertainment.

SIXTH HOUSE: Labor, the condition under which work is done, tenants, food, small animals, employees and the quality of their services, and illness.

SEVENTH HOUSE: Marriage, partnership, the attitude of those met in public, open enemies, competitors and law suits.

EIGHTH HOUSE: Gifts and legacies, the public's money, ability of those owing one money to pay, death and the influence of those dead.

NINTH HOUSE: Teaching, publishing, advertising, lecturing, long journeys, religion and the court.

TENTH HOUSE: Honor, business, credit, profession and superiors.

ELEVENTH HOUSE: Friends, hopes and wishes.

TWELFTH HOUSE: Crime, sorrows, dissappointments, restrictions, hidden enemies, large animals, unseen forces and astral entities.

The Tenth House—Because the tenth house is more closely associated with vocations in general than any other house, it should receive special discussion; in fact, the whole Trinity of Wealth, embracing the job itself as ruled by the tenth house, the conditions under which the actual work is done, ruled by the sixth house, and the money received, ruled by the second house, need to have their functions somewhat clarified.

It seems reasonable to expect a planet in the tenth, or ruling its cusp, to have more influence over the vocation than does a planet of equal prominence elsewhere located in the birth-chart; for the thought-cells it thus maps are directly related in the unconscious mind with credit, honor, business and position. And this seems to be borne out by our studies of these 3,000 vocational charts.

This, however, is quite different from implying that the ruler of the cusp of the tenth or a planet in the tenth can be considered a constant for any of these vocations. To be sure, a planet in the tenth or ruling its cusp, has more power to determine the vocation than a planet of the same prominence not a ruler of the tenth; but that power is so slightly more in determining the vocation that its consideration has small practical value. Just as our analysis of the Sun-sign, Moon-sign and Ascendant-sign indicate that there are more with certain of these signs prominent who follow a given vocation, yet that this predominance is not marked enough to be a constant, or deciding factor in any vocation, and therefore should be given secondary consideration; so in the 30 vocations here covered, we have found in the analysis of each series of 100 charts covering a given vocation, some with each of the twelve signs on the cusp of the tenth, and some with each of the ten planets in the tenth, and none there often enough to be considered a constant, or to warrant such tenth house influence being given more than secondary consideration.

Because the ruler of the tenth maps thought-cells which in the astral body are closely associated with business, honor, credit and position, there often is a tendency, or leaning toward following a vocation signified by it. But unless the ruler of the tenth has prominence, which means that it maps thought-cell activity, and consequently ability of that planetary type, the individual does not make a success of that calling, and eventually must turn to some other vocation in which he has greater ability. Which means that it is foolish for an individual to attempt to follow a vocation indicated by the tenth house if the ruler of the tenth has so little prominence that it is clear he has no ability of that kind.

Ability, as has been emphasized, is due to accumulated experiences of a definite type built into the thought-cells of the astral body, and mapped in the birth-chart by houses and planets. And a planet in the tenth house denotes no more experience and no greater thought-cell activity, and consequently no greater natural aptitude for work of the kind denoted by the planet, than does the same planet in the first house. A planet in the tenth house, practically devoid of aspects, denotes less thought-cell activity of its type, and consequently less natural aptitude of that planetary type, than a planet in the seventh, fourth or first which is powerfully aspected. The ruler of the tenth in a cadent house and not aspecting Sun, Moon or Mercury, and not making other powerful aspects, denotes the individual is so lacking in ability of that planetary nature that he could not make a success of it.

The tenth house, as well as each of the other houses, does have an outstanding significance. The thought-cells it maps are those which have been built into the soul by experiences which relate to that which man calls credit, business and position. Thus a planet in the tenth house, or ruling its cusp, is significant of the conditions the individual will encounter, no matter what vocation he follows, that influence his credit and position.

For instance: Politics and politicians are ruled by the Sun.

Professor Nicholas Murray Butler, President of Columbia University since 1902, has the Sun and Neptune in the tenth. He has been Chairman of the Republican National Convention at various times, and otherwise known for his political interests, but politics is not his vocation. Neither is Admiral Richard E. Byrd a professional politicians. But the Sun in the tenth house of his birth-chart enabled him to gain the aid of those in political authority, without which his explorations covering both poles of the earth would have been impossible.

Both David Lloyd George and Howard Jones have the Moon in the tenth house of their charts. Both had a tremendous popular following, and the doings of both were of keen interest to a vast number of people. Lloyd George was the Premier of the British Government during World War I, and Howard Jones was a famous football coach.

Stephen Foster, the composer of Old Black Joe, My Old Kentucky Home, and other American folk songs, had Mercury and Venus in the tenth. Mercury was afflicted, and he had strenuous opposition to his determination to write music. Marconi was not a writer, but an inventor. Mercury was in his tenth house; and the radio which he invented, was used to send messages, ruled by Mercury.

Henry Ford has Venus and Saturn in his tenth house. Neither the inventions nor the manufacturing for which he is noted are ruled by one of these planets, but his reputation among some people is as beneficient and mild as Venus, and among others that of slave driving Saturn. Jean Harlow, the movie star, had Venus, the Moon and Saturn in the tenth. She had the Venus reputation as a glamour girl, the fan public indicated by the Moon, and career difficulties characteristic of the hardships of Saturn.

Professor A. Vander Nailen, internationally known physicist, had Jupiter and Neptune in the tenth. He had a fine reputation in his profession, but his interest in mysticism (Neptune) brought cynical smiles from his engineering friends. Dr. Alexis Carrel, famous Member of the Rockefeller Institute for Medical Research, has Sagittarius on the cusp of the unoccupied tenth, and its ruler, Jupiter, conjunction the Moon in the house of medicine (sixth).

Adolph Hitler has Saturn in the tenth. Napoleon had Saturn, Mercury and the Sun in the tenth. The reputations of both are associated not merely with ambition, but also with hardships undergone by people due to their leadership. Jack London, the writer of adventure fiction, had Venus and Saturn in the tenth.

So far as his fiction writing is concerned his reputation was aptly described by Venus; but for his materialistic philosophy and economic views his career severly suffered.

Jane Addams, of Hull House fame, had the Moon and Uranus in the tenth house. The common people among whom she worked, and the wide interest of people in her work, is indicated by the Moon. But the reform character of her efforts, and the unusual way she went about it, are indicated by Uranus. Major Edward Bowes, who first put non-commercial broadcasting on the air, and has conducted amateur radio programs resulting in the discovery of many people of talent, has Uranus in the tenth. The avenue through which he works, and the groups with whom he co-operates, are denoted by Pluto in the seventh; but the original methods he has introduced into his business are indicated by tenth house Uranus.

Marge Gestring, who became woman diving champion of the world at 13 years of age, has Mars in the fourth and Jupiter rising to give love of athletic sports, and ability in them. But it was her ability to dramatize her ability that caused schoolmates to furnish the money to send her to Berlin where she won the championship. Huey P. Long, with Jupiter and Pluto also in the tenth house, had Neptune there; and no politician on record has had greater ability to dramatize himself.

Pluto is the planet of dictatorship and also the planet of universal welfare. Huey P. Long, with Pluto, Jupiter and Neptune, in the tenth, became the dictator of Louisiana. He told other politicians what to do and they did it. Jupiter in the tenth enabled him to manipulate people of wealth. Upton Sinclair also has Pluto in the tenth. But he has worked consistently for socialism and production for use. An outstanding writer, he has made it his business to expose corruption; working to the best of his ability for universal welfare.

None of the nine planets I have thus far mentioned in the tenth house of notable people have been the constants of the chief vocation they followed. But the planet in the tenth has had an influence upon the success of their careers. And any planet in the tenth, or ruling the cusp of the tenth, does have an influence over the career, even though the business or profession followed may be chiefly ruled by a prominent planet, or planets, not in the tenth or ruling its cusp. To indicate what I mean, for it is definitely important that this should be understood, I have selected the planet Mars in the tenth house. And the charts of those selected as illustrative of this point will all be those of people, as were those already mentioned, whose hour of birth is known, whose erected charts are published with comments in Brotherhood of Light Lessons, and with whose lives every person should be familiar.

Douglas Fairbanks, Sr. had Mars in his tenth, and his athletic screen acting, as well as the criticism of his life and honor, were of the Mars type. In the world of music, Ben Bernie has Mars thus located, and anyone who has listened to the music of the "Jazz King" at once detects the Mars quality; and it can also be discerned in his relations with various employers. Ann Morrow Lindbergh, who does some writing, has Mars in the tenth, and has illustrated its power through the hazardous flights she has taken with her husband. A truly outstanding writer with Mars in the tenth is James Branch Cabell. The unconventionality of some of his works, such as Jurgen, brought acrimonious controversy and violent criticism.

At opposite poles, it is easy to think, are a killer who was hanged for murder and a Supreme Court Justice. Albert Dyer, with Mars in the tenth, gained national notoriety for strangling three little girls. When Hugo L. Black, with Mars in the tenth, was appointed Supreme Court Justice, a violent controversy split the nation. He won senate confirmation by the barest margin. Commerce, exploration and religion have to do primarily with the ninth house. Henry M. Stanley, famous African explorer had Mars in the ninth house, but in less than one degree from conjunction the M.C.; Daniel C. Roper, who was Secretary of Commerce for the U. S., had Mars in the tenth house; and Aimee Semple McPherson, famous evangelist, has Mars in her tenth. All three at various times in their lives were subjects of violent controversy and acid criticism.

There is probably no point in carrying these illustrations much further. It is possible to go on and mention mechanics, waiters, telephone operators, and those who follow each of the 30 vocations here considered, who have Mars in the tenth house, and about whose position and credit there has been strife and criticism. Not to neglect the politicians, it may be mentioned that both Calvin Coolidge, who called out the military to put down a Boston police strike, and later was President of the U. S., and Franklin Delano Roosevelt, who was President when the U. S. entered World War II, have Mars in the tenth. Both have been severely criticized, and both had to fight valiantly in their political careers.

What here has been pointed out in some detail relative to

Mars is equally true of each of the other nine planets, as I have illustrated more briefly, in indicating its own characteristic type of conditions affecting the credit and position of any individual in whose birth-chart it is in the tenth house. That is, a planet in the tenth house affects the credit, honor, position and business in almost the same way it affects the home when in the fourth house, affects the condition of work when in the sixth house, affects the finances when in the second house, or affects any other house in which it is found. And to a less marked degree a planet also affects in its characteristic manner the house bearing on its cusp the sign which it rules.

I am not advocating that in selecting a vocation either the tenth house and its ruler, or the signs occupied by Sun, Moon and Ascendant be completely ignored, merely pointing out that these cannot be considered constants of any vocation so far analyzed; for a large majority of those in any vocation will be found to violate any rules that may be laid down in reference to these positions. These positions do, however, within the vocation which is followed, whatever it may be, have a significance, such as I have pointed out, well worth observing.

The M.C., Asc., Sixth House and Second House—Each aspect in the chart of birth maps a stellar aerial in the astral body which picks up and radiates astral energy. And some of this astral energy is brought to a focus in the region of the astral body mapped by the apex of the birth-chart. Clairvoyantly the M.C. is marked through the astral body by a sharp blue line. And all such energy, whatever its character may be, which reaches this line, is widely broadcast. The sharp blue line mapped by the degree on the M.C. acts as an amplifyer.

Because the various aerials mapped by aspects in the birth-chart remain throughout life, except as changed through conditioning by events after birth, they are called permanent aerials. But in addition to the permanent aerials, or stellar wires, across the astral body, which persist, there are others which form temporarily.

When a planet makes an aspect by progression, either to the place of a planet in the birth-chart, or to the place of another progressed planet, there is formed within the astral body a thread of astral substance connecting these two points. That is, the progressed aspects map temporary aerials that form and dissolve within the astral body. They are temporary, but while they last they pick up and transmit the energy of the two planets making the aspect to the thought-cells in the astral body, greatly increasing their activity. It is due to this increased activity that the thought-cells are able to attract events into the life.

This book is not the place to treat of progressed aspects. But they must be mentioned in connection with vocations, and in connection with the M.C., because sometimes a progressed aspect is operative at birth and continues operative much or all of the life. And when this is the case the thought-cells mapped at either end of the aspect have as great activity during much or all of the life as the thought-cells of other people do during those limited periods when progressed aspects form.

The statistics we have compiled from the analysis of 2,700 charts erected for known birth hours and progressed to the time of some event in the life of the individual, prove that events of any consequence to the individual only take place when there is a major progressed aspect heavier than that from the Moon, within about a degree of perfect—although occasionally when Sun or Mars is involved and there are other heavy progressed aspects operating, a degree and a half must be allowed—to the ruler of the house mapping the department of the life affected. And the analysis of the progressed aspects at the time of these 2,700 dated events also proves that both the M.C. and the Asc. must be handled, both in respect to progressed aspects made to them in the chart of birth, and in respect to the aspects they make by progression, as if they were planets; but that none of the cusps of the other ten houses react thus to progressed aspects, or to the progressed aspects they make to the planets.

Any planet in the birth-chart making an aspect to the M.C. maps thought-cells whose energies have facilities, by way of the aerial leading thus to the M.C., for getting public recognition. Reaching the M.C. thus they are amplified and broadcast, and more people learn about the things they have influenced than learn about other qualities of greater significance which do not thus connect up with the M.C.

When two planets in the birth-chart are within one degree of the perfect aspect they make a progressed aspect. And so long as this aspect lasts the thought-cells thus mapped have unusual activity. Thus progressed aspects lasting from birth through much of the life indicate planets of great prominence, and thought-cells of much power. And if there is such a permanent progressed aspect from a planet to the M.C., it indicates that all through life there is the utmost facility for getting public recognition for the quality indicated by the planet.

To indicate what I mean; Henry Ford has 12 Virgo 00 on the M.C. and Pluto in 12 Taurus 10. Progressed Pluto throughout his life does not move a full degree from 12 Taurus 10, and therefore is trine birth-chart M.C. by progression permanently. Pluto is the planet of mass production, and is in the house of labor (sixth). Henry Ford had done other things of note, but that for which he has received the greatest publicity is the development of mass production and his relation to his employees.

President Franklin Delano Roosevelt has 11 Gemini 45 on the M.C. and the Sun in 11 Aquarius 04. At first glance it might be assumed that the Sun is not powerful enough to make a successful politician, even though conjunction Venus and square Neptune, Saturn and Jupiter. But at second glance this impression is dispelled; for not only is the Sun trine birth-chart M.C., but as the M.C. and Sun progress by identical amounts, progressed Sun is trine progressed M.C. throughout life. That is, he at all times has Sun thought-cell activity as great and as fortunate as most other politicians do at such a favored three years of their lives as progressed Sun comes to the trine of the birth-chart M.C. He is the first President to be elected for a third term.

In addition to planetary aerials and the blue line marking the M.C., the clairvoyant discerns a heavy line running across the astral body in the region marking the sign and degree on the Ascendant in the birth-chart. This may be compared to a ground wire, in that it is where the person connects, and exchanges energy through his electromagnetic forces, with his immediate physical environment. In some vocations personality, as well as ability, is important. And in gauging the personality, and how it will affect other people, not only should planets in the first and ruling its cusp be considered, but aspects to the ascending degree. Quite different from the M.C. amplifyer, this ground wire of the personality reaches in its influence only so far as the electromagnetic emanations flow. But in so far as personal contacts are concerned, every aspect to the Asc. has some significance.

The tenth house is the position, or job. The sixth house is the actual work, and the conditions contacted during the work, while engaged on the job. Saturn in the sixth house attracts laborious work and disagreeable surroundings while doing it, Mars brings strife to the work, Jupiter attracts those who are helpful, etc. We analyzed the progressed aspects in the charts of 100 people when they secured employment, and the charts of 100 people when they lost employment. All 100 had both a progressed aspect to the ruler of the tenth and a progressed aspect to the ruler of the sixth at the time they were employed. All 100 had a progressed aspect to the ruler of the sixth at the time they lost their jobs, and 97 of them at that time also had a progressed aspect to the ruler of the tenth. It is easier to get a job when the ruler of the tenth and the ruler of the sixth are afflicted by progression than when no progressed aspect forms to them.

The second house represents the money acquired or lost. It is not essential to have a birth-chart aspect from the planet ruling the vocation to the planet ruling the second house. But if there is such an aspect it connects up the vocational activity with the money thought-cells and makes it easier for them to influence money matters than if no such aspect were present.

The Zodiacal Signs Indicate the Particular Approach to Work —In each series of 100 birth-charts of those following a certain vocation, the signs in which were found the Sun, Moon and Ascendant were tabulated. And whenever there was shown a significant tendency for a particular sign to qualify in the work, or a decided tendency for a particular sign to avoid the work, this has been indicated immediately following the tables of planetary prominence and house activity. It has been found exceptional, rather than the rule, for some signs to run 30% above the average, or 30% below the average. Often the variation was so little as to warrant no mention of it. In none of the 30 vocations analyzed can any sign be considered a constant of the vocation, or any sign be considered as prohibiting the individual from engaging in the vocation. People may, and do, successfully follow any of these 30 vocations regardless of the sign occupied by the Sun, Moon, Ascendant or planets. Furthermore, no matter what signs are occupied by the Sun, Moon, Ascendant or planets, people may, and do, succeed in the occupation who have the planets and houses which are the birth-chart constants of the vocation prominent.

What the signs do indicate are not the natural aptitudes required by certain vocations, but the particular approach and handling of the work for which the prominence of certain planets and the activity of certain houses show the qualifications. In this manner, and in this order of importance, can knowledge of the signs occupied by the Sun, Moon and Ascendant be utilized.

In general, the movable signs, Aries, Cancer, Libra and Capricorn can break trails for others to follow, and start enterprises that others finish. They are the pioneers. People born under the mutable signs, Gemini, Virgo, Sagittarius and Pisces seldom break trails, but follow on the heels of the pioneers. They are the developers. But for work requiring close attention to detail, the fixed signs, Taurus, Leo, Scorpio and Aquarius are better suited. They have great resistance to pressure of all kinds, strong endurance and plodding perseverance. They are not originators, and not enthusiastic developers; but when development has reached a high degree they can work out the details that constitute improvements. They are the perfectors.

This is an age of specialization. People are not just machinists. They are ignition experts, die makers, auto repair men, etc. And in the selection of the specialization within the field covered by the natural aptitudes as shown by the prominent planets and active houses, the signs can be used to advantage. For instance:

ARIES is never content unless he is something of a leader. In almost every vocation there is opportunity to start something new, or to start in a new vicinity. He likes the zest of competition.

TAURUS is very reliable and efficient in taking care of other people's possessions. He does not like change; but once he learns to do something in a particular way he will continue to do it in that manner.

GEMINI is restless and can do many things well. But unless given opportunity for change and variety he is apt to grow restless and quit his job. He also likes plenty of opportunity to talk.

CANCER is quite sensitive to his environment. The fear of ridicule is torture to him and often prevents him from asserting himself to advantage. He should associate with people who are sympathetic.

LEO has a thirst for authority. He is better at deputizing work than at taking orders from others. Other people usually respond to his faith in them by endeavoring to live up to his expectations.

VIRGO often is a walking encyclopedia of information. He has keen discrimination, and often becomes exceptionally valuable to executives who do planning, for he can find the weaknesses and how to strengthen.

LIBRA needs to meet people personally. He dislikes to get his hands or clothing dirty. He is a lover of harmony, and so dislikes to hurt another's feelings that he can seldom say no.

SCORPIO is resourceful and does not flinch either from trouble or disagreeable tasks. He is intense in his likes and dislikes and whatever he finds to do he does with his whole might.

SAGITTARIUS can both give and take orders. He goes straight to the mark, caring more for effectiveness than elegance. He needs open air recreation, and plenty of opportunity for mental activity.

CAPRICORN is methodical, ambitious and diplomatic, with a faculty for organization and bringing together dissenting factions.

He should have some opportunity for management in whatever he does.

AQUARIUS understands human nature better than any other sign. He likes to keep posted on the newest ideas and developments, and knows just what to say and do to produce a given effect on other people.

PISCES is sensitive and much influenced by environment. He should be thoroughly interested in and enthusiastic about his choice of work. He needs an atmosphere of sympathy and encouragement.

Chapter Three

THE INFLUENCE OF CONDITIONING AND ENVIRONMENT

There are just five things which should receive consideration in selecting a vocation in the following order of importance: 1. The natural aptitudes as indicated by the prominent planets and active houses of the birth-chart. 2. The luck attracting power of the associations amid which the aptitudes may with advantage be employed, as indicated by the aspects of the various planets. 3. The previous conditioning, including education and training, of the individual. 4. The environmental conditions under which he will be compelled to follow the vocation. 5. The progressed aspects operative in his chart during the time he follows the vocation. The first two have already been discussed. So now let us consider the other three and any minor matters that have a bearing upon vocational selection.

The positions of the planets at any given time indicate the direction in which their energies are flowing and combining with other planetary currents. The sum total of these streams and their convergences form an inner-plane pattern. And when proper physical conditions also are present, souls can be born in human form who correspond in the broader features of their thought-cell organization to the planetary pattern at that time, although they may vary considerably from this pattern in detail.

But to fit the birth-chart pattern it is only necessary that the thought-cell organization resemble the astrological pattern in the relative activity of each thought-cell group to other thought-cell groups, relative to the harmonies and discords of the thought-cells, and relative to all other structural proportions in the astral form. It is not necessary that there shall be any particular volume of thought-cell activity in the astral form considered as a whole. In other words, while the relations and comparative volumes of the energies are shown by the birth-chart, the total volume of energy acquired from experience may be several times as much in one individual's astral form as in another's, even though they are born at the same moment and practically the same place.

No one can determine from looking at a chart whether it is the birth-chart of a mollusk, the birth-chart of a reptile, the birth-chart of a bird, the birth-chart of a dog, or the birth-chart of a man. But on its own evolutionary level each of these creatures will exhibit the traits and attract the events signified by its birth-chart. At least horses, dogs and cats do; as we have experimented rather extensively with their charts.

But our researches have not stopped there. We have compared the lives of astrological twins, born of different parents, but with almost identical birth-charts. And we have compared the accomplishments of different people with the significant planet, so far as we could determine, equally prominent in their charts, and having similar aspects. And while relative to the accomplishment signified by other planets in the same chart there is apt to be a close parallel, the amount of accomplishment of one may be several times that of the other.

The student need only compare the birth-charts of people in his own community with the birth-charts of famous people, to find charts quite similar to those of famous persons, of people who have exercised similar talents and attained some local prominence, but who have gone not nearly so far.

The chart of a draft horse may show him to be very speedy. But even so, he will be outdistanced in a race by almost any horse of the racehorse strain. The draft horse is speedy only in comparison to other draft horses. And thus it is also with men and women. From the birth-chart alone can only be determined the amount of natural aptitude an individual has of a particular type in comparison to his other natural aptitudes; and not the extent of the success he can make using this natural aptitude in comparison to the success some other person can make in the same vocation. To appraise how great a success he can make relative to some other person with similar birth-chart positions, it would be necessary to know the evolutionary level of both. This factor, which is not shown astrologically, has been given the letter (G) on the Astro-Physical Interaction diagram.

However, this evolutionary level (G) is of no significance in the selection of a vocation. In selecting the best vocation which an individual can follow, we are not trying to determine how great a success he can make in the vocation. Instead, we are determining, relative to such ability and fortune-attracting thought-cells as the individual has, in which particular vocation he can be more successful than in other vocations, be that success large or be it small.

But there are two factors, other than those mapped in the birth-chart (A) or indicated by progressed aspects (C and D), that are of great significance. They are the special conditioning by events since birth, and the resistance offered by physical environment, indicated by letters (B) and (E) on the Astro-Physical Interaction diagram.

The Influence of Environment—As the thought-cells have been built by the states of consciousness resulting from experiences with environment; and as the desires of these thought-cells and therefore what they strive to do has been determined by the pleasure or pain of such experiences; it is apparent that contact with environment in pre-human life-forms is largely responsible for the inner-plane organization mapped by the chart of birth, and that experiences after human birth continue to add energy which builds thought-cells in the astral body, to add energy to existing thought-cells, and to change the desires of thought-cells that already form a part of the soul.

This giving direction to the desires of the thought-cells is called conditioning. And as soon as it occurs, every experience with environment has an influence upon the way some of the thought-cells are conditioned. That is, it tends to modify their desires and consequently the manner in which they try to influence the behavior and the events that come into the life. Thus we cannot separate conditioning from the influence of environment. But, at least before the individual has reacted to it, we can separate environment from conditioning. Also we can consider environment apart from the energy it adds to certain thought-cells as affording facilities for certain events and offering resistance to others. And it is a grave mistake to overlook environment in the selection of a vocation.

Age is a portion of the environment. After the vocation has been selected, it is never too early to begin to think about the best method of conditioning—training—the individual for the occupation. But environmental demands make it impossible for those too young to follow certain vocations, and make it difficult, or perhaps impossible, for those beyond a certain age to obtain employment in them. And environmental demands may make it very difficult for a person of one sex to gain employment in a vocation on which the opposite sex has a virtual monopoly. Both the age and the sex are indicated by the data furnished for the chart of birth.

But quite aside from such data, during some periods there are environmental demands for those who follow certain vocations that are not present during other periods. During the first fifteen years of the present century, for instance, there was a constant and vigorous demand for teamsters. But the demand for those with ability to handle work horses has since given way to the demand for those with ability to drive motor trucks. No matter how much natural aptitude for teaming birth-charts may indicate, few people at the present time should be encouraged to become teamsters.

At the time this is written the United States has become the arsenal of democracy, and has committed itself to all-out production of war materials. For the time being it is difficult to get employment in anything that does not contribute to the war effort. But there is a tremendous demand for those skilled in the use of machine tools. And to my personal knowledge there are those drawing big wages in the aircraft industry, doing routine work well enough after a period of training, who have very little natural aptitude for mechanics. They have far greater ability for some other vocation; but the demand for aircraft workers at present is so great that they are making more money, and serving their country better, than if they engaged in any other type of work.

When the radio became popular it decreased the demand for a certain type of musician. The Federal Housing Project created a special demand for carpenters and plumbers during the half decade before the U. S. entered World War II. But for the whole decade previous to this war there was a repletion of white collar workers which persists to the present time. The demand has been for those who can work with their hands. However, automobile workers are not in demand just now, and hundreds of thousands of those previously engaged in the auto factories are out of employment while undergoing training to fit them for war production work. Furthermore, there is usually a constant demand for those following certain vocations, such as telephone operators and salesman, and an uncertain demand for those following others, such as professional athletes and professional dancers.

In selecting the vocation, therefore, due to environmental conditions, it may be better for the individual to train to follow some occupation for which there is a demand, even though he has a little more aptitude for some other, than to follow the special one for which most suited. I am not implying that the great poets, musicians, writers and inventors who have almost starved to death that they might contribute something of high value to society, should have followed some other work. Merely that the price which an individual must often pay to work at something for which there is no commercial demand should not be overlooked.

Progressed Aspects Should Receive Consideration—Referring to the Astro-Physical Interaction diagram, in selecting the best vocation to follow, (A), (B) and (E) are all factors that require attention. And if there is also a time element for its commencement, or for its practice, we must also consider factors (C) and (D).

What I mean is that if at a particular period in an individual's life he desires to take up some vocation for which his birth-chart indicates a natural aptitude, it is well to examine the progressed aspects at the time to determine how such work, or the attempt to get into it, will affect him at this particular period. It may be that, due to heavy progressed afflictions at the time which would find in the vocation full opportunity to attract disaster, it would be unwise for him to enter a vocation at one particular time of life in which he would be unusually successful at other times.

We have made a point of collecting the birth data of pilots and others who have cracked up in airplane disasters. In all we have obtained up to the present time, there was a heavy progressed aspect to Mars at the time of the crash. Often a pilot has flown a commercial plane for years without accident, and then when exceptionally heavy progressed afflictions have formed in his chart, including a heavy aspect to Mars, he has run into the top of a mountain, or made a disastrous forced landing. During some special period in the life of an individual whose chart normally shows great success in aviation, there may be such progressed afflictions to Mars, Uranus and Saturn that aviation during this period would have a high probability of disaster by accident. Such conditions would be shown by (C) and (D).

On the other hand, the progressed aspects operative during a given period of the life may well so favor following a specific vocation that there would be greater gain from it during this period than from some other vocation for which there is better natural aptitude, but toward which the progressed aspects at the time were highly unfavorable.

Only under certain unusual circumstances is an individual warranted in following a vocation for which he has no natural aptitude; but there are often indicated in the birth-chart a variety of natural aptitudes which are less outstanding than those indicating the best vocation. And if either the physical environment (E), or the progressed aspects (C and D), or both, during a given period of the life specially favor a vocation for which there is some aptitude, even if it is not the one for which there is most aptitude, it may be better during this period to turn the attention to the vocation thus favored.

In the selection of vocations for children, (B) often can largely be controlled; that is, the child can be conditioned in the direction which will most aid him in making a success of the chosen vocation. But even in selecting a vocation for a child, the progressed aspects (C and D) which will be operative at the time he can be expected to commence following it on his own, should not be ignored; nor should (E) the demand for such services and the hazards or other conditions they will stimulate in the life be left out of consideration. A vocation when it is actually practiced, or the attempt made to practice it, comes under all the rules that are generally applicable to events.

Employer or Employee?—It frequently happens that a person who is unusually successful in handling a business for another is able to earn a very nice salary; but as soon as he goes into business for himself he loses all he has. On the other hand, a person who makes very little success in the employ of others often is able to make a marked success when he breaks away from such servitude and establishes himself independently. This is important in vocational matters, and is determined chiefly by three birth-chart indications.

1. The first of these is the tenth house. I have already indicated that the thought-cell activity mapped by the tenth house affects the business, credit and honor, and that the line marked by the M.C. acts as an amplifyer. Any thought-cells mapped by the tenth house have ready access to this amplifying device, and thus get publicity.

As a general rule, the more elevated a planet is in the chart, that is, the closer it is to the cusp of the M.C., the more readily the qualities represented by the thought-cells it maps get publicity. But as affecting the honor and business in particular, any planet aspecting the cusp of the tenth, or aspecting a planet in the tenth, and thus mapping a stellar aerial reaching to the amplifyer, is more important than a planet elevated and not in the tenth.

If, therefore, the ruler of the tenth house, and the cusp of the tenth (the amplifier), are well aspected, it is an excellent indication that the person can make a success in business for himself. But if planets in the tenth, the cusp of the tenth, or the ruler of the cusp of the tenth, receive discordant aspects, it indicates difficulties that tend to hamper an independent business.

2. An individual may be in business, or may follow a profession,

without the aid of employees. Even so, as he is the center about which the business revolves, it is well to have the Sun thought-cells powerful. If these are weak and discordant, as indicated by a Sun not prominent but afflicted in the birth-chart, his power of control over the business tends toward disorganization and failure. But this is more important in proportion as the activities of other persons must be directed in the business, especially if such direction must be made through personal contact. To boss others successfully the Sun needs prominence, and if well aspected there will be less difficulty attracted in this effort.

3. From the purely financial angle, the two business planets, Jupiter and Saturn, are of more importance than the Sun. Where buying, selling, bargaining and sound business judgment are concerned, the thought-cells mapped by these two planets must be relied upon. If they are weak and discordant they indicate lack of business ability; but to the extent they are active and harmonious do they indicate both judgment and the so-called luck which contribute to financial success.

When these three factors of business success—the tenth house, the Sun, and the two business planets—are weak and much afflicted, it is better for the individual to follow his vocation in the employ of others. As there seems to be no limit to the salary it is possible to command, if the abilities are pronounced enough, this need be no hardship. But if the three factors mentioned are favorable, he can with advantage go into business for himself.

The Best Vocation—The general rule for selecting the best vocation is first to determine the most pronounced natural aptitudes. This is done by noting the most prominent planets and the most active houses, without regard to whether the aspects involved are harmonious or discordant. Vocations employing the natural aptitudes thus determined have been ascertained statistically, and can be selected from the vocational analyses given in this book. And from the requirements of these vocations which have actually been analyzed, and from the type of ability indicated by each of the planets as hereafter shown, it should not be difficult to select the natural aptitudes and the birth-chart positions mapping them, for almost any other vocations.

After having selected the natural aptitudes—for an individual can use only the kind of ability he possesses—the next thing is to determine amid what associations he should employ these aptitudes to attract the most good fortune. The harmony or discord of a planet determines the luck attracted in an environment ruled by it. The best planet in the chart, which means that it must be prominent as well as harmoniously aspected, indicates the most fortunate environment. And the house whose ruler, or rulers, is harmonious, indicates a department of life in which good fortune is easily attracted.

As an ideal, the best vocation for an individual is one which permits his greatest natural aptitudes to express amid the surroundings ruled by the best planet in his birth-chart. But often conditioning (B) or environment (E), and sometimes even the progressed aspects at a given time (C and D) make it advisable to compromise on something a bit short of this ideal. An individual may find it expedient to neglect the use of some one of his outstanding aptitudes, or to use his greatest aptitudes amid associations that are not as harmonious as those indicated by his best planet and best birth-chart houses.

The Influence of Conditioning—It has already been indicated that as soon as the consciousness of the individual reacts to it, every experience with environment adds energy to some of the thought-cells within the astral body, giving them more energy and influencing the direction of their desires, and therefore how they will affect the behavior and how they will strive to attract events into the life in the future. This, however, is only part of the story. The balance of it shows indisputably that two people with practically identical birth-charts, if reared amid environments which afford facilities for different kinds of events, have their thought-cells so conditioned by this divergence of experiences that they have quite different destinies, and the events attracted into their lives under the influence of the same progressed aspect may be different in the department of life chiefly affected, in their importance to the individual, and in the amount of fortune or misfortune; although in each instance the events will bear the characteristics of the planets making the aspect and belong to a house ruled by one of the planets involved in the aspect.

Professional psychologists have found that identical twins reared in separate homes have different I.Q.'s. The University of Iowa's Child Welfare Research Station, investigating the result of orphans born of feeble-minded parents being adopted by highly intelligent families, found their average I.Q. was 115, well above normal (100). Not one was dull. Concluded the Station's director, Dr. George Dinsmore Stoddard: "With good upbringing even a dull child may become bright."

Our CASE HISTORY STUDIES of Identical Twins, Natural Twins and Astrological Twins who have almost identical charts also indicate that the environment is a powerful factor in conditioning the thought-cells to desire certain events of their planetary type rather than other events of the same planetary type, and that the reaction to these events which the environment affords with facility, also tends to influence the importance of the events attracted later, and the relative degree of good fortune or misfortune.

As an illustration, we published such a CASE HISTORY, embracing the analysis of 25 astrological influences, chiefly progressed aspects, as affecting the lives of Douglas Fairbanks Sr. and his Astrological Twin, in the seven issues of THE RISING STAR commencing with the August 3, 1940, issue. Fairbanks had 17 Aries on the M.C. and 1 Leo 13 rising. The Twin had 19 Aries on the M.C. and 4 Leo 12 rising. The only planet in a different house was the Moon.

Of the 25 events which coincided with the same progressed aspects or other astrological influences in both lives, the planetary characteristic was the same in each pair of events; the house rulership was different in only 16% of the events, although the events in all cases belonged to a house ruled by one of the planets involved in the progressed aspect; there was a difference in the fortune of the events in 32%; a difference in their importance in 28%; and the specific events differed in 68%. Of these differences in the events attracted in these two almost identical birth-charts by similar progressed aspects, we attributed 12% to the differences that existed between the birth-charts; 32% due to an additional progressed aspect operating in one chart at the time of the event which was not present in the other; 32% due to difference in the physical environment at the time the event took place; and 60% due to different conditioning by earlier environment.

All the 25 events or conditions were similar enough to demonstrate to an unprejudiced mind the power of progressed aspects to attract events characteristic of the planets involved and the houses these planets rule. But what we are interested in here is that such differences as have been found to exist in their lives were 60% due to differences in earlier environment. And CASE HISTORY studies of the charts and events in the lives of natural twins and identical twins show a similar power of early conditioning to divert the life and change the specific nature, the importance and the harmony or discord, of the events attracted.

In the case of Natural Twins of Opposite Sex, in which 15 similar sets of astrological influences were analyzed in the five issues of THE RISING STAR, commencing April 7, 1940, the differences in the events attracted were 67% attributed to conditioning, which was half again as much as that attributed to birth-chart differences including sex, which is part of the birth-chart.

Fairbanks' father was a lawyer who habitually declaimed Shakespeare in the home. Fairbanks became saturated with drama in his childhood. The Astrological Twin was reared in an atmosphere of mechanics. His father and uncle owned a blacksmith shop. One expressed his tenth house Mars in daring and athletic acting, the other chiefly working with machines.

Education and training, whatever it may be, is conditioning. A person who has not become familiar with a musical instrument at maturity will never become famous as a pianist, because his fingers have become too inflexible. A job requiring a college education is not suitable to a person who without getting it has passed the years for acquiring such an education. Always, in selecting a vocation, the background of training and education should be considered.

I believe the most important knowledge astrology affords is that while the type of energy of the thought-cells mapped by a given planet cannot be changed, it can be diverted into any one of numerous channels of expression. No one can make Saturn thought-cells influence the behavior to become aggressive, or to work to attract the Mars type of events; but it is possible to train Saturn thought-cells that have influenced the individual to be self-centered and pessimistic, and have repeatedly attracted loss into his life, to influence him to find satisfaction in system, order and organization, and to attract responsibility. And it is possible to train Mars thought-cells that have influenced the individual to be irritable and belligerent, and have repeatedly attracted accidents, so that they will influence him to think constructively, and work to attract constructive enterprises into his life.

After the thought-cells have expressed their particular type of energy in a certain trend of thought and behavior a few times, they form the habit-system of expressing in a similar way. At any stage of life such habit systems, due to conditioning, can be changed. But the earlier in life such effort is made the easier it is. To enable such conditioning to be attempted intelligently, especially in reference to vocational matters, before taking up in alphabetical order the actual analysis and requirements relating to each of 30 vocations, it seems well to point out some of the experiences that formed the thought-cells mapped by each planet in the birth-chart, and to indicate channels through which each can be trained to express by conditioning after human birth.

SUN: Throughout its evolutionary past the soul has had some contact with other life-forms and the members of its own species. And at all stages before human birth, as well as after being born into human form, the ability to exercise authority has carried with it certain advantages.

In the animal world, for instance, ability to exercise authority enables a creature to dominate territory and thus more adequately secure a supply of food. It enables it to secure the mate of its choice, and to prevent the mate being stolen by a rival. And when community life is established, this Drive for Significance becomes more than the mere seeking of food and reproduction. It becomes the desire to have the respect of, and to be obeyed by, others. Thus a herd of wild horses is ruled with tyranny by some stallion which has vanquished all rivals, and migrating geese look to some wise old gander for leadership.

All experiences which have been associated with the exercise of authority have built Power thought-elements into the finer body. The normal degree of activity of the thought-cells so formed is indicated by the prominence of the Sun in the chart of birth. And only those with these Sun thought-cells quite active have a natural aptitude for work where the exercise of authority is essential.

These Sun thought-cells cannot be too active; but it is easy for them to become so discordant they cause endless trouble. Properly to condition them, the individual should early learn that undue assumption of superiority really weakens his authority, and that consideration of the opinions of others and sympathy with their views will tend toward getting better service. In other words, he should learn to find satisfaction in getting people to want to do as he desires them to do, rather than in forcing his will upon them.

Not only a politician, but a shop foreman, a floor walker in a department store, the head of a department, and others under whose supervision people work, need active Sun thought-cells.

MOON: To provide sustenance and comfort for the young is one of the most commonly observed activities among most forms of life. Plants exercise the utmost ingenuity to see to it their seeds are carried by wind, or water, or in the fur of animals, to a place where the environment will favor their growth. Birds weave intricate nests, and animals construct dens and lairs, to secure safety for their offspring; and all will fight to the death, and endure amazing hardship and peril, for them.

Such experiences in housing and rearing the progeny built the Domestic thought-elements into the finer body. The normal degree of activity of the thought-cells so formed is indicated by the prominence of the Moon in the chart of birth. And only those with these Moon thought-cells quite active have a natural aptitude for music, for contacting the common people, or for caring for the weak and helpless.

Some people with the Moon prominent take to music as naturally as do some birds and some insects. But to become successful as a musician, the individual needs training, and the earlier this conditioning is started the better. By maturity the fingers are usually too inflexible to start becoming an instrumental musician. Professional dancers also, who express the domestic melody in rhythmic motion, need to start training early.

Cosmeticians, waiters, store clerks and telephone operators must have the Moon thought-cells active to enable them to meet the general public; and should condition themselves to find pleasure in giving all types of people satisfactory service.

Farmers and nurses and others whose success depends on their ability to care for the young or the helpless, need a prominent birth-chart Moon. And they should early condition these Moon thought-cells to get their highest satisfaction from bringing young plants or animals to sturdy maturity, or from bringing back to health those who are ill.

MERCURY: Insects, birds and mammals find it of advantage to be alert, to perceive enemy or food quickly, to remember where their homes or sources of food are, to be able to select proper material for home building, and to do whatever they need to do with dexterity.

Such experiences in the exercise of alertness, dexterity, memory and perception built the Intellectual thought-elements into the finer body. The normal degree of activity of the thought-cells so formed is indicated by the prominence of Mercury in the birth-chart. And Mercury—because it is never over 28 degrees from the Sun, and Venus is never over 45 degrees from the Sun, and consequently Mercury is frequently conjunction Sun or Venus, and moving faster than the other planets, makes many other aspects—is prominent more often than any other planet. Also the Mercury thought-cells are important in more vocations than any other thought-cells.

They are needed in setting down lines, words or figures by architects, artists, draftsmen, bookkeepers and stenographers; in problem solving by some of these and by astrologers, chemists, electricians, machinists, and radio technicians; in giving ability to talk or otherwise express ideas clearly by lawyers, movie stars, politicians, salesmen, teachers and writers; to give memory or dexterity to dancers, dentists, store clerks, telephone operators, and waiters; to give alertness to such of these as serve the public; and the intelligence to be versatile and adaptable where these qualities are required.

But as cleverness with figures, writing, practicing law, etc., are not abilities of lower life-forms; the adaptability of the individual at maturity to follow such a vocation depends largely on the channels into which during early life the energy of the Mercury thought-cells have been conditioned to flow. They may have been conditioned to neglect mathematics and find satisfaction in the use of language, or they may have turned their energy chiefly into channels of alertness. In other words, at a given period of life, the specific trend of ability given by the Mercury thought-cells largely depends upon the previous education.

VENUS: Some plants bear staminate and pistillate blossoms on different individuals; yet other plants, such as those of the primrose family, have male and female associated in a single flower. Some animals have no social life except at mating time, and others, such as the eagle and the ostrich among birds, and the lion and the beaver among mammals, mate for life.

Experiences with companionship and mating in lower forms of life have built Social thought-elements into the finer body. The normal degree of activity of the thought-cells so formed is indicated by the prominence of Venus in the chart of birth. And only those with these Venus thought-cells quite active have a natural aptitude for work where neatness, harmony, grace, beauty, or artistic expression is essential.

Even those with active Venus thought-cells need proper conditioning early in life to divert the Venus energy into artistic expression. Birds of some species build artistic homes, and dance at mating time. They also posture and display themselves, and give forth joyous music. But even so, to express beauty as an architect, artist, cosmetician or even the taste required by a dentist, needs considerable training, as does the neatness of a draftsman.

The musician needs to cultivate the Venus sense of harmony, the professional dancer must add grace of movement to harmony, the musician must train his muscles and his ears, and the movie star must learn to increase the Venus attractiveness of his personal appearance. Without an environment which affords opportunity for training the thought-cells to express in channels giving vocational ability, the Venus thought-cells, however active they may be, are apt to express nearly all their energy in affectional and social channels.

MARS: Every life-form, if it is to survive, must be able to meet and defeat enemies from which it cannot escape. To acquire food there must be incessant activity, and to overcome obstacles imposed by changing environment rather than perish, requires initiative. The demand to reproduce the species develops amativeness.

Experience with combat, with overcoming obstacles, with taking the initiative, and with love making in lower forms of life have built Aggressive thought-elements into the finer body. The normal degree of activity of the thought-cells so formed is indicated by the prominence of Mars in the chart of birth. And only those with these Mars thought-cells quite active have a natural aptitude for outstanding muscular activity, for combat, for handling machinery, for taking the initiative, for mathematics, for building, or for creative work of any kind.

Whether the Mars thought-cells when active give a talent for mathematics or mechanics, for soldering or doctoring, for quarrelsomeness and combat, or for constructing bridges and buildings, depends largely on the facilities of early environment to condition them to find satisfaction in one of these expressions. The same individual with Mars and certain other planets prominent may become a movie star or a good mechanic.

The athlete, the dancer and the waiter need the muscular activity of Mars. The bookkeeper, chemist, engineer and architect need active Mars thought-cells for mathematics. The aviator, mechanic, radio technician and electrician need them for mechanical ability. The doctor, nurse, architect, draftsman, dentist, artist and cosmetician must have the Mars constructive ability. The policeman must have Mars daring, and the movie star must have the Mars initiative to beat down obstacles.

JUPITER: Even many lower forms of life place implicit faith in their parents. And among gregarious animals the confidence in the leader to protect and find ample for their need becomes the beginning of hope. Reverence and veneration develop through obedience to such ruling authority, and looking to such higher power for guidance, protection and satisfaction of wants. To acquire the favor of the leader, or higher authority, the spirit of tolerance toward other members of the group is cultivated.

Various experiences in lower forms of life, in which tolerance and good will have taken part, and in which there was confidence in higher authority, have built Religious thought-elements into the finer body. The normal degree of activity of the thought-cells so formed is indicated by the prominence of Jupiter in the chart of birth. And only those with these Jupiter thought-cells quite active have a natural aptitude for such professions and occupations as depend on the patronage and good will of others.

To become a professional athlete these good fellowship thought-cells must become conditioned to find satisfaction in sports. The dentist, the doctor, the lawyer and the politician must have them conditioned to find satisfaction in professional activity, and in their power to attract patronage and good will. The store clerk and the salesman should have them so conditioned that he finds great satisfaction in inducing people to like him well enough to come to him for purchases.

SATURN: One of the outstanding abilities of all life-forms which survive is that which enables them to avoid harmful conditions and consequent destruction. Deer flee when pursued by wolves, and squirrels and bees store food for winter.

Experiences with fear, caution, acquisition, greed, system and selfish wants in lower forms of life have built Safety thought-elements into the finer body. The normal degree of activity of the thought-cells so formed is indicated by the prominence of Saturn in the chart of birth. And only those with these Saturn thought-cells quite active have a natural aptitude for those vocations requiring persistence, system, order, organization, management, shrewd buying, planning, or painstaking, routine or laborious work.

The architect and engineer need Saturn thought-cell activity for planning structures. The lawyer needs them to organize his evidence and plan the most effective presentation. The bookkeeper needs them to enable him to give system to his work. The store clerk and the policeman need them to enable them to follow routine duties without becoming restless. The dentist needs them to attract teeth, which Saturn rules; and the machinist needs them to enable him to do painstaking work. The musician needs them to enable him to stick with the long hours of practice, day after day, which are required to become skilled, and the farmer needs them to hold him to the plodding and laborious work of his occupation.

Early conditioning them to find satisfaction in responsibility and effective management is a help when these qualities must be used later in some vocation.

URANUS: As environment is constantly changing, the ability to make marked departures from previous customs has enabled many species to survive that otherwise would have become extinct. When the ordinary food supply became exhausted through flood or drought, for instance, ability to depart radically from the old food habits were highly advantageous. And when the authority exercised by the flock leader restricted opportunity for reproduction, rebellion against authority may have been beneficial.

Experiences with ingenuity, with original conduct, and rebellion against precedence and authority in lower forms of life have built Individualistic thought-elements into the finer body. The normal degree of activity of the thought-cells so formed is indicated by the prominence of Uranus in the chart of birth. And only those with these Uranus thought-cells quite active have a natural aptitude for powerfully influencing the conduct of others, or for work where originality, inventiveness, the use of new ideas or radical departures from established custom is required, or the use of electricity.

The electrician, telephone operator and radio technician need active Uranus thought-cells to attract them to electricity and handle its gadgets. The lawyer, politician and salesman need them to be able to influence others. The aviator, engineer, chemist and machinist need their inventive ability, and aptitude in handling gadgets. The architect and movie star need them for originality. The stenographer needs them to enable short cuts to be made, and the astrologer needs them to attract him to an unusual pursuit, and to give an interest in the influence of the stars.

If the Uranus thought-cells are early given opportunity for constructive original work this usually prevents them from expressing in rebellion and eccentricity later.

NEPTUNE: All creatures draw from their inner-plane experiences certain impulses which cause them to strive for a more satisfying type of life. Animals other than man also have dreams, and many creatures gain information through feeling extra-sensory perception.

Such experiences, in which mental escape has been made from the harsh restraining walls of reality to a realm devoid of hardship, have built Utopian thought-elements into the finer body. The normal degree of activity of the thought-cells so formed is indicated by the prominence of Neptune in the chart of birth. And only those with these Neptune thought-cells quite active have a natural aptitude for work which requires promotion, unusual schemes, psychic work, impersonal friendliness, dramatization, great imagination, or the handling of poisons.

The professional athlete, dancer, cosmetician, movie star, musician or artist must be able to dramatize his own personality, the personality of others, or the work he does. The extra-sensory perception given by active Neptune thought-cells are a pronounced aid to the psychic and the astrologer. The aviator must have them to attract him to aviation, which is ruled by Neptune. The policeman must have them if he is successful in laying traps for law breakers. The waiter needs them to give the necessary impersonal friendliness and attitude of servitude. The architect and draftsman need them to the extent imagination is required in their work, and the chemist must have them to attract him to the poisonous chemicals he handles.

As active Neptune thought-cells give the individual the inclination to seek the line of least resistance, their energy readily is conditioned to express in day dreaming, in idealistic visions about which nothing is done, in futile dramatization of schemes which are impractical, and in various forms of escape from reality. It is essential, therefore, that the individual with active Neptune thought-cells should, as early as possible, be trained to express their energy through the use of imagination or the dramatic talents in channels that bring concrete results. That is, all introspective and negative processes should be discouraged, and the individual trained to find satisfaction in creative imagination, that is, in the use of imagination for actual accomplishment.

PLUTO: Specialization of parts and division of labor are to be found not only among the cells and organs of each organic creature, but among the members of many plant and animal communities. The colorful flowers, for instance, display gorgeous petals or sepals as advertisements to attract insects to the nectar secreted by certain cells, and thus insure the pollination and reproduction which are the work of other specialized parts. Bees and ants and beavers co-operate for the welfare of the community in home building, and in storing food for use during winter.

Experiences which have been associated with co-operation, with coercion, with group activities or with invisible forces have built Universal Welfare thought-elements into the finer body. The normal degree of activity of the thought-cells so formed is indicated by the prominence of Pluto in the chart of birth. And only those with these Pluto thought-cells quite active have a natural aptitude for working with groups, for co-operation, for understanding hidden forces, for mass production, or for universal welfare work.

The astrologer, the electrician, the chemist, the occultist and the radio technician need these thought-cells active to enable them to understand the invisible forces with which they work. The dancer and the policeman need them active to give ability for co-operation. The waiter, the store clerk, the telephone operator and the politician need them active to enable them to handle people in groups or many people in a short time. The farmer, the statistician and the production line manufacturer need them active to give ability in mass production. And the nurse needs them active to give the desire to work for universal welfare in the care of those ill.

Chapter Four

ASTROLOGICAL CONSTANTS AND STATISTICAL ANALYSIS OF 30 VOCATIONS

While in this book only 30 different vocations are analyzed by the statistical method of selecting the most constant factors in the timed birth-charts of people who follow them, its usefulness is intended to extend to all vocations. A little thought based on what is said in this book will indicate the type of natural aptitudes required to follow any vocation, and therefore just which planets must be prominent and just which houses must be active to indicate these aptitudes. The last half of chapter three and the analyses of the vocations which form this chapter should make it comparatively easy thus to select the astrological constants indicating the thought-cell activity giving any required aptitudes.

It should, of course, be understood when I refer under each vocation to *The Luck Factor,* that I am not implying good fortune or bad fortune without an adequate cause. That which is called good luck or bad luck is the result of the activity of harmonious thought-cells or discordant thought-cells. But to avoid endlessly repeating this explanation, I shall refer to it merely as *The Luck Factor;* just as for convenience astrologers refer to Sun and Moon as planets, knowing full well one is a star and the other a satellite.

A study of the luck attracting power of the associations amid which the 30 vocations here analyzed may with advantage be employed will give a background for deciding what the luck attracting associations should be for an individual with given planets harmonious and given planets discordant, whose aptitudes are those for any vocation not here considered.

The other three of the five factors that should receive attention in the selection of a vocation—previous conditioning, present environmental conditions, and the individual's progressed aspects—are as easily appraised relative to other vocations as to these here analyzed, and in the selection of any vocation must be considered on their individual merits.

The statistical analysis and comments that follow, therefore, while applying specifically to the vocations of which we have been able to obtain 100 charts of those following each, are by no means confined in their usefulness to so limited a field. Instead, they should afford a reliable statistical basis on which the advisability of following any vocation, whatever it may be, can be determined.

ARCHITECT

Birth-charts of architects analyzed	100	100%
Charts with Saturn prominent	100	100%
Charts with Mercury prominent	100	100%
Charts with Neptune prominent	99	99%
Charts with Mars prominent	99	99%
Charts with Venus prominent	97	97%
Charts with Uranus prominent	95	95%

Third House Activity of 100 Architects

Charts with third house active	95	95%
Charts with planet in third house	57	57%
Charts with third house more discordant than harmonious	72	72%
Charts with third house more harmonious than discordant	26	26%

Fourth House Activity of 100 Architects

Charts with fourth house active	98	98%
Charts with planet in fourth house	59	59%
Charts with fourth house more discordant than harmonious	73	73%
Charts with fourth house more harmonious than discordant	25	25%

A tabulation of the 100 charts according to signs occupied by Sun, Moon and Ascendant gave Leo highest, Scorpio next, then came Cancer, Virgo and Libra. Pisces and Aries were lowest with only about half as many as Leo.

There are no doubt two distinct reasons why Saturn is constantly prominent in the charts of architects. One is that Saturn is the planet of planning, and an architect's work consists chiefly in planning various kinds of structures. The careful attention to innumerable details, the necessity that every item shall occupy exactly its proper place relative to every other item, and the painstaking estimates of the ability of materials to stand up under a given stress, all call upon active Saturn thought-cells.

The other reason is that Saturn is general ruler of structures and the land on which they rest. For one to be interested sufficiently in buildings to be drawn into association with them as a vocation would seem to require both active Saturn thought-cells and active fourth-house thought-cells. The fourth house maps the common thought-cells relating more specifically to the department of life having to do with buildings of all kinds.

Not only do the plans of the architect require plodding and painstaking work; but in the calculation of stresses, of the suitability of material, of the cost of the materials to be used, and the exact amounts of various items required, there is call upon mathematical ability. The study required to become an architect, and the cerebral activity employed in the work, make calls upon the thought-cell activity mapped by Mercury. But in addition, the mathematical part of the work makes calls upon abilities which Mars thought-cells and Mercury thought-cells together provide.

Constructive work of any kind needs active Mars thought-cells. But mathematical ability requires both active Mars thought-cells and active Mercury thought-cells. And in so far as these two planets are concerned, they are even more essential to an architect than to a draftsman; for in addition to the skill in the use of drafting tools which they give, there is also required a higher degree of mathematical ability, and more constructive energy of the type which Mars alone affords.

There is also greater call upon the imagination, which Neptune rules. The architect must be able to visualize how a building or other structure will look when completed. And he cannot merely visualize what someone else has created, he must be able to employ creative imagination in a high degree. The creative energy is furnished by Mars, and the imagination by Neptune.

In its broader application Mars is the planet of creative energy. That is, it furnishes the energy to build dams, skyscrapers, dwellings, and machines. But for creative energy to flow persistently into artistic work of any kind the Venus thought-cells also must be active. Active Venus thought-cells alone give an appreciation of beauty, and confer good taste where appearances are concerned; but alone they do not create anything. For artistic creation of any kind, including that of an architect, there must be active gonad glands, the hormones of which give a creative urge beyond that required by the ordinary needs of human life.

Venus and Mars are closely associated in their rulership over the gonad glands. Their influence is not easily separated. But when both are prominent, and especially when closely in aspect to each other, their thought-cell activity stimulates the secretion of the gonad hormone, which acting upon the nerves generates electromagnetic energy of the frequency employed by the affectional system. And this electromagnetic energy gives both the urge and the power for artistic creation.

Such artistic expression may take the form of selecting certain beauties from nature and reproducing them. But if the Neptune thought-cells also are active, the imagination not merely selects certain more obvious things for its composition, but also explores the inner plane, even though the individual is unaware he is thus employing the extra-sensory perception which active Neptune thought-cells give. His intense creative urge extends his consciousness beyond that which the physical senses can report to gather material. The unconscious mind leaves no stone unturned either on the physical plane or the inner plane to acquire proper material for the creative work attempted, and to bring it together in pleasing effect.

In greater degree than the draftsman, the architect, in addition to creative imagination, must possess the good taste mapped by a prominent Venus. The appreciation of harmony is an activity of the Venus thought-cells. The draftsman requires such taste merely to induce him to keep his drawings neat. But the architect, in addition, must be able to visualize harmony in the structure he plans.

Originality of any kind depends upon the activity of the Uranus thought-cells. And as an architect's work requires originality, the invention of new designs, which a draftsman's work does not, he must have the Uranus thought-cells more active. People with active Saturn thought-cells can make plans based on what others already have done. They have thoroughness and system. But unless there are also active Uranus thought-cells they will never design anything new. The creative imagination supported by active Neptune thought-cells gives visions of beauty; but for the actual inventive ability an architect needs, the Uranus thought-cells should be active.

As his work calls for placing on paper his estimates and drawings, to make this department of life significant enough to attract him to such work, he also needs active third house thought-cells.

The Luck Factor—An architect's work, unlike that of a mere draftsman, makes Mercury and the third house incidental to planning, which is ruled by Saturn, and to structures, which are ruled by the fourth house. His work thus primarily is ruled by Saturn, and in determining his luck while following it, we should look first of all to how Saturn is aspected. Primarily, to the extent, and from those quarters indicated by harmonious aspects to Saturn, will good fortune help him in this vocation.

Secondarily, as the success of the completed structures is a determinant of success in the long run, the good fortune or ill fortune—as distinct from ability—is indicated by the harmony or discord of the fourth house thought-cells. Yet among practicing architects, nearly three fourths of them offset with ability a fourth house more discordant than harmonious. This means that they follow the profession of their choice in spite of adversities encountered.

ARTIST

Birth-charts of artists analyzed	100	100%
Charts with Venus prominent	99	99%
Charts with Mars prominent	99	99%
Charts with Neptune prominent	96	96%
Charts with Mercury prominent	94	94%
Charts with Venus aspecting Moon or Mercury	91	91%
Charts with Mars aspecting Moon or Mercury	91	91%
Charts with Venus aspecting Mars	66	66%

A tabulation of the 100 charts according to the signs occupied by the Sun, Moon and Ascendant gave Gemini the highest, with Libra and Sagittarius next highest. The lowest numbers were found in Aries, Taurus and Aquarius, each of which had just two thirds as many as either Libra or Sagittarius. Even so, if the planetary constants are shown, there is no justification in discouraging a person from becoming an artist simply because his Sun, Moon and Ascendant are in signs which hold fewer artists than some of the others.

Those who succeed as artists usually have the ability to think clearly about things. They have ideas or impressions which they desire to express as accurately as possible on canvas, and in the manner which most completely will transfer them to the minds of those who look at their work. I speak of painting here because, with the exception of a few commercial artists, practically all the 100 charts analyzed were those of painters. And in painting, the material selected to be included requires the exercise of such critical intelligence as is afforded by active Mercury thought-cells. The painter needs not merely the artistic sense to feel when he has produced the effect he desires, but also ability to think deeply and make proper selection of what should go into, and what should be left out of, his composition. Furthermore, he should have the manual dexterity which a prominent Mercury gives. Thus, while not so important as some of the other factors, active Mercury thought-cells are a decided advantage to an artist.

The accurate reproduction of an object or scene usually is not considered art. A camera thus can be made to represent actual physical conditions. Art requires selectivity, as already mentioned in connection with Mercury, and the combination of the selected material in such a way as to dramatize something. Through selectivity and artistic combination of material the picture must be more beautiful than the original, or it must emphasize some factor and suppress others in a manner that will convey to the observer the conception or feeling which the artist wishes to impart.

Art to be successful must dramatize. And whether in business or in art in any of its various forms, including painting, when dramatic talent must be employed, the promoter or artist to be successful must possess active thought-cells such as are mapped by Neptune in his chart of birth. Not only moving picture stars, writers of fiction, and musicians, need Neptune prominent in their charts of birth, but those in all other fields of artistic endeavor.

But while it includes the exercise of Mercury intelligence and Neptune dramatic appreciation, artistic work is essentially an expression of creative energy. Those who do not possess creative energy cannot express it. An individual can use only what he has. The ordinary conditions of everyday life, including the domestic relations, make some call upon creative energy. But beyond developing sufficient creative energy to fulfill such ordinary needs of human life, to be creative as an artist the individual must develope more than the normal intensity and volume of creative energy. This means that he must have a glandular make-up such that he generates electrical energies of tremendous power which radiate electromagnetic wave-lengths of the type most readily used by the affectional system.

To generate this type of electromagnetic power there must be strong and active gonad glands, such as are ruled by Venus and Mars. Mars and Venus are too closely associated in their influence upon the sex function to be able to separate their influences as affecting the gonad glands. Yet it is quite proper to speak of Venus as the planet of love and affection and Mars as the planet of energy and passion, to point out that the thyroid gland on which normal energy production depends reacts not only to the Sun but also to Venus, and that the glands of emergency energy, the adrenals, react not merely to Saturn but equally as vigorously to Mars.

In its broader application Mars is the planet of creative energy. It is used to give the doctor the desire and ability to heal. It is used by the engineer in the drawing of plans and the building of bridges, dams and skyscrapers. It is used by the soldier to enable him to destroy, and by the law-enforcement officer in meeting the force of the criminal with superior force and helping build a more secure society. Wherever initiative and the destruction or the building of something are required, the glandular makeup necessary calls for active gonads and ample adrenalin.

But for the creative energy to flow persistently not merely into sporadic passion and cerebral and physical activity, but into the affectional system, the glandular reactions produced by the Venus vibrations must be sufficient to divert the creative energy into this particular electrical system of the human constitution. And to do this the planet Venus must be prominent in the chart of birth.

The electromagnetic energies radiated by this Venus type of activity may be long or short, and the potential varies greatly, but they do have the quality of supporting intense feeling and encouraging some expression of love. Love is capable of expression on an innumerable number of levels. Under the dominion of the selfish propensities of Mars it expresses as lust. On a higher level it expresses as the marital attraction between husband and wife, and as the affection for children and friends. Some intensely love the birds and the trees and the flowers. The appreciation of a gorgeous sunset or the majesty of a mighty waterfall is an expression of the love nature. Ecstacy and religious fervor are sublimations of the same energies even though they require the action of either Neptune or Jupiter to make the sublimation possible.

To be able to create there must be ample Mars energy. To be able to appreciate beauty there must be ample Venus energy. To be able to create beauty there must be both ample Mars energy and ample Venus energy. It takes adequate Venus energy to divert the energy of Mars into channels which relate to beauty. As both Venus and Mars have a powerful influence over the gonads, an aspect between these two planets is the best indication that strong electrical energies—in some individuals so strong that it controls them—of the affectional system surge over their nerves. The Moon or Mercury aspecting these planets facilitates the expression in forms of art.

The Luck Factor—As Venus rules art in general and painting in particular, the harmony or discord of the thought-cells mapped by Venus are significant of the tendency to attract luck in association with artistic work. However, a harmonious planet in the chart, especially if it makes a favorable aspect with Venus, may indicate some special association amid which more luck would be attracted.

If Venus made a harmonious aspect to a planet in the ninth, for instance, it would signify that art work in connection with books or periodicals would be fortunate. Magazine covers or advertising thus would be indicated as fortunate associations. Or if there were a good aspect between Venus and the ruler of the fifth house, or the fifth house and Neptune were fortunate in the chart, the artist would be lucky doing art work for theatres or the moving picture industry. Saturn well aspected in the chart, or harmoniously aspecting Venus, would indicate luck in interior decorating; and Jupiter well aspected in the chart, or harmoniously aspecting Venus, would indicate ability to attract the patronage of wealthy people.

ASTROLOGER

Birth-charts of astrologers analyzed	100	100%
Charts with Uranus prominent	100	100%
Charts with Neptune or Pluto prominent	100	100%
Charts with Mercury prominent	94	94%
Charts with Pluto prominent	92	92%
Charts with Neptune prominent	86	86%

We also tabulated the signs in these charts occupied by the Sun, Moon and Ascendant; but none of them stood out from the others sufficiently to warrant it being given special mention, and certainly no sign can be considered a birth-chart constant of astrologers.

To the extent the upper-octave planets Uranus, Neptune and Pluto are prominent in a birth-chart is the individual easily interested in things out of the ordinary, including psychic matters and astrology. Not all of those who have one or more of the upper-octave planets prominent become interested in astrology, however. Some with Uranus prominent use the energy of these thought-cells in oratory or in legal practice, in engineering, in invention, or in some other form of originality. Some with Neptune prominent use the energy of the Neptune thought-cells in dramatic work or in promoting something quite apart from occult work. And some with Pluto prominent use its thought-cell energy in becoming gangsters, or leaders in some constructive work where co-operation is required.

Yet those who seriously engage in any occult pursuit, such as astrology, metaphysics, or spiritual healing, always have at least one, and usually at least two, of the upper-octave planets prominent in their charts of birth.

Uranus is the planet of astrology. This means that the thought-cells mapped by the planet Uranus must have considerable activity if an individual is to become interested in astrology. And, other things being equal, the more active the Uranus thought-cells are, the greater the chance that the individual will be attracted to astrology.

While it is extremely unlikely that a person in whose chart Uranus is not prominent will become an astrologer; yet some of the best known promoters of astrology have had Neptune far more prominent in their charts—often in the tenth house—than Uranus. In these cases there may have been merely a close aspect of Sun, Moon or Mercury to Uranus, and Uranus not in an angle. This was sufficient, however, to enable the individual to become conversant with astrological practice. And thus conversant with it, the still more powerful Neptune thought-cells enabled him to promote astrology on a vast scale; where others of perhaps much greater astrological ability were able to become only slightly known, and did correspondingly little for the spread of valuable astrological information.

In astrology, as in other professions, the ability to attract patronage is to quite an extent dependent upon the activity of the thought-cells mapped by Jupiter. And thus in the analysis of these 100 charts of astrologers, it was found that those who follow it as a profession, and with some degree of success, almost invariably also have a prominent birth-chart Jupiter.

There are a great many people who believe in astrology, and would like to know more about it, who never become astrologers. Usually they have Uranus prominent, or at least some of the upper-octave planets prominent; but lack the necessary intellectual application to become proficient in the subject. If Uranus is prominent enough, this may make up for the lack of a prominent Mercury, as the table indicates. But usually only those with the Intellectual thought-cells active, as mapped by a prominent birth-chart Mercury, are studious enough to become astrologers.

The Pluto thought-cells tend to give an interest in all types of invisible forces, including those received from the planets. They thus favor an interest in all occult subjects; and when they are directed into constructive channels, they incline to use all such invisible energies for the advancement of mankind.

Among astrologers, in addition to those who are able to give good astrological readings from following the rules and their own observation of what chart positions commonly indicate, there are two other outstanding types.

One of these has the Mars thought-cells active, usually Mars in close aspect to Mercury, or at least aspecting the Moon. Uranus may be quite prominent, and usually is. These aspects of Mars give facility in mathematics. And those who have weak Mars and Mercury thought-cells often have great difficulty learning to erect a chart and work out the progressed aspects. But at the other extreme are some of those who have Mars and Mercury quite prominent, who are unusually proficient in mathematics, but who can, seemingly, never learn to read a chart. Commonly this type devotes much energy to working out difficult and complicated theories based on mathematics; but is quite unreliable in delineating from these theories, or from those more commonly accepted.

The other pronounced type is the person who has Neptune a dominant influence in his chart, and not sufficient Uranus, Mars and Mercury to give a desire for even the simplest work with figures. These people have made a habit of getting things the easy way; through the use of their psychic faculties. Often they seem quite to lack the ability, or with others the initiative, to learn to erect a birth-chart and work out the progressed aspects from which alone a scientific delineation and forecast can be made.

Yet these people often give readings which are amazingly correct from a chart someone else has erected. More commonly than not they have little concise knowledge of the rules of scientific astrology, and vary the reading according to the way they feel. They can always point to some planet or position as responsible for what they say will take place; but on different occasions will attribute quite opposite tendencies to the same astrological position. These people, who invariably have a prominent Neptune, and Uranus perhaps just prominent enough to interest them in astrology, are not scientific astrologers. They merely tune in on the individual through the avenue of the birth-chart and progressed aspects, and depend upon feeling extra-sensory perception to give them the information they desire. Yet, often, the readings they give are amazingly correct.

Thus, in addition to the typically Uranian astrologers, there are mathematical astrologers, and there are psychic astrologers. And it is a very valuable thing for the truly scientific Uranian astrologer to have sufficient of the Mars-Mercury or Mars-Moon influence to be able to handle the mathematics of his work with facility. Also it is quite valuable for him to have Neptune prominent enough to enable him to pick, through his psychic impressions, the particular event among several that might be expected to be attracted under a given progressed aspect.

While it is true that extremes of the mathematical type, and extremes of the psychic type, are not the most desirable astrologers; yet there can be no doubt that some ability along mathematical and psychic lines is an advantage. Also, that thought-cells mapped by a prominent Pluto assist to understand how the planetary energies operate, and what to expect from them. Thus in addition to mathematical ability enough to set up a chart and work progressed aspects, the best indications of ability are to have all three upper-octave planets prominent.

The Luck Factor—As astrology is essentially ruled by Uranus, the general fortune attracted in association with it is indicated by the aspects to Uranus. In its practice, however, it is customary to interview clients, and the clients are ruled by the seventh house. The luck with clients in general must be appraised from the aspects to the ruler of the seventh. If the third is a fortunate house, and the first badly afflicted, more fortune is indicated through a mail order practice; as the discordant personality will then not have facilities for bringing about disagreeable events. The well aspected planets in the chart indicate the types of clients from whom the most luck may be expected in the practice of astrology; especially any planets favorably aspecting Uranus.

ATHLETE

Birth-charts of athletes analyzed	100	100%
Charts with Mars prominent	99	99%
Charts with Jupiter prominent	98	98%
Charts with Neptune prominent	98	98%
Charts with Mercury prominent	95	95%
Charts with Mars aspecting Jupiter	59	59%

First House Activity of 100 Athletes

Charts with first house active	97	97%
Charts with planet in first house	53	53%
Charts with first house more discordant than harmonious	54	54%
Charts with first house more harmonious than discordant	44	44%

Fifth House Activity of 100 Athletes

Charts with fifth house active	96	96%
Charts with planet in fifth house	55	55%
Charts with fifth house more discordant than harmonious	53	53%
Charts with fifth house more harmonious than discordant	42	42%

A tabulation of the 100 charts according to signs occupied by Sun, Moon and Ascendant gave Virgo highest, with Sagittarius having almost as many. Cancer was lowest, Capricorn next lowest, and Aries with only one more than Capricorn and two more than Cancer; Cancer having a little more than half as many as Virgo.

Neither the number of planets in the first house nor the number in the fifth house can be considered significant. In these same charts 54 show planets in the eighth house and 60 planets in the twelfth. However, the absent rulers of these two houses are powerfully enough aspected to make the first house and the fifth house significant.

The element of personality does not seem so pronounced as

that of store clerks, in whose charts 62% had planets in the first house. But it does seem that the physical body, which is more closely related to the first house than to any other, must have the activity indicated by strong aspects to its ruler.

The house ruling sports and amusements of all kinds is the fifth. It seems that to be attracted powerfully enough to sports to make the effort to excel in them requires, not planets in the fifth, but the amount of fifth-house thought-cell activity mapped by its ruler being strongly aspected.

The factor in the tabulation which was not anticipated is the prominence of Neptune. At first the thought occured that this may have been influenced by the fact that quite a number of those whose charts were analyzed in this group had been connected with the movies, which Neptune rules.

However, in addition to dramatic talent, we have found that Neptune is strongly associated with amusements of all kinds. People frequently take vacations, or temporarily withdraw from the more utilitarian pursuits of life, under progressed aspects to Neptune. It thus seems to have an affinity for recreation of all sorts.

Furthermore, the athlete who becomes outstanding—and the charts used were mostly of professionals and amateurs who had attained considerable recognition—must have some promotional ability. Most of those who attain eminence in athletics, either with an amateur standing or professionally, have considerable ability to dramatize their talents.

Sports in general come under the rulership of Jupiter. Not only athletics, but horse racing and sailing contests. The seriousness of Saturn, untempered by Jupiter, considers such events a waste of good time and energy. Jupiter likes to laugh, to meet his fellows in a playful mood, and is quite willing to spend time and money on that which gives him enjoyment. Venus is not adverse to having a good time; but does so less boisterously than does Jupiter. Social events, dancing, music, the arts and not too vigorous indoor amusements, are typical of Venus. But Jupiter needs more action and less daintiness to give him a good time. Not only the liking for sports, but the good fellowship of those engaged in it and of those attending sporting events, are evidences of the influence of Jupiter; in fact, that which commonly is called "good sportsmanship" is an expression of the Jupiterian spirit of fair play and willingness to abide by the rules even if the cost is great.

But associated with sports there has come to be also, at times, an atmosphere which is not Jupiterian. If we consider good sportsmanship an expression of Jupiter, we are warranted, I believe, in attributing "fixed" prize fights, "fixed" horse races, "fixed" baseball games, and such concealed machinations of sports events, to the scheming qualities of Neptune. Such events are promotions of the Neptune confidence-man type.

So far as muscular ability is concerned, we must look chiefly to the prominence of the planet Mars. It not only gives strength and agility to the muscles, but furnishes energy of the high voltage type which is so necessary for violent action. In other words, Mars is the planet ruling athletes. But the other planets indicated in the table also must be prominent; otherwise the individual may express his Mars not in athletics, but in mechanical or engineering lines. And many an individual who, if he had Jupiter, Neptune and the fifth house sufficiently active to give him a love for sports, could make a champion, is quite content to handle tools or build skyscrapers.

Intelligence is of various kinds. Some relates to understanding science, some to expressing thought in speech or writing, and some to other lines of endeavor. In most vocations it is an advantage to have Mercury prominent in the birth-chart.

Athletic supremacy is not merely a matter of brawn. It also requires quick perception and ability intelligently to adapt to swiftly changing conditions. A baseball player or one engaged in teamwork sports of any kind, must be able to size up instantly a situation involving many others, and act upon the decision then made. Prize fighting and wrestling requires fast and sound headwork. It should not be surprising, therefore, to find that Mercury is usually prominent in the charts of those who succeed in athletics; and that when Mercury is not prominent the planet Uranus is.

The Luck Factor—Where strife is present, even the friendly strife of athletics, Mars thought-cells are important. And as Mars is the primary ruler of athletics, as distinct from the other types of sports, we should look to the aspects of Mars to determine the general luck attracted in association with athletics. Those with heavy Mars afflictions, especially at the time progressed aspects form to Mars, are those with a tendency to become injured while engaged in athletics.

While Mars is the more important factor in determining the general luck attracted in association with athletics; the luck attracted while associated with sports in general is only less significant. And in determining this, give about equal weight to the aspects of the planet Jupiter, planetary ruler of sports, and to the aspects of the ruler of the fifth house, which is the house of sports. It is to be noted that the analysis shows the fifth house more often than not more discordant than harmonious. Jupiter also is more often more discordant than harmonious. Even one favorable aspect to Jupiter and one favorable aspect to the ruler of the fifth is a great help, and may enable an athlete of outstanding ability to gain recognition.

AVIATOR

Birth-charts of aviators analyzed. 100   100%
Charts with Neptune prominent. 99   99%
Charts with Mars prominent. 96   96%
Charts with Uranus prominent.. 94   94%

Ninth House Activity of 100 Aviators

Charts with ninth house active 98   98%
Charts with planet in ninth house. 57   57%
Charts with ninth house more discordant than harmonious 56   56%
Charts with ninth house more harmonious than discordant 40   40%

Third House Activity of 100 Aviators

Charts with third house active   95   95%
Charts with planet in third house...... 41   41%
Charts with third house more discordant than harmonious 67   67%
Charts with third house more harmonious than discordant 28   28%

We tabulated the signs in which the Sun, Moon and Ascendant were located in these charts, but none of them were outstanding enough to warrant special mention; and certainly none can be considered the birth-chart constant of aviators.

Not only in reference to its prominence in aviators' charts, but in reference to world and national events in which aviation has played an important part, the dates on which outstanding flights have been undertaken, and the progressed aspects in aviators' charts when they undertook important flights, we have been able to check the rulership of aviation. There at present can remain no doubt that Neptune is the planet ruling this vocation, and flying in general. Even as a prominent Neptune in business signifies that the sky is the limit, so among occupations it is even more literally so.

While most of the unusually important flights have been made when the aviator was under a progressed aspect to Neptune, this is not true of all of them. For instance, in 1924, James H. Doolittle made the first Dawn to Dark flight across the U. S. under progressed Sun P Neptune. In the first round the world flight, Lieutenant Smith, commander of the fleet of Navy planes, was under progressed Venus trine progressed Neptune. Admiral Byrd was first to fly across the North Pole in 1926, while he was under the influence of progressed Mars trine birth-chart Neptune. He crossed the Atlantic in 1927 under progressed Mars trine progressed Neptune; but having run out of Neptune progressions, he flew over the South Pole in 1929 under the influence of progressed Venus square Uranus.

Of the two charts tabulated in which the ninth house ruler was not powerfully aspected, one of these is that of Anne Morrow Lindbergh, the ruler of whose third house is in the tenth and powerfully aspected. Captain Charles Lindbergh on his famous New York to Paris flight was not under a progressed aspect to Neptune; but under progressed Mercury sextile Uranus. Amelia Earhart, the first woman to fly the Atlantic, however, had Venus progressed to the semi-sextile of Neptune when she made that flight; and Captain Hugo Eckner made the first Zeppelin flight around the world in 1929 when the progressed Sun came opposition birth-chart Neptune. Even in a later around the world flight record, that of Post and Gatty, making the trip in less than nine days, while we do not have the data for Gatty, we find that Wiley Post, the pilot, was under progressed Mars P Neptune.

Wiley Post later, along with the famous humorist, Will Rogers, perished in Alaska on a pioneering flight to route an airway to Siberia, while under heavy progressed afflictions to Mars; and Amelia Earhart perished in the Pacific in 1937, on a round the world trip, while under unusually heavy progressed afflictions from Mars. On January 11, 1938, the giant Samoan Clipper burned in mid-air, dropping bits of wreckage and the charred bodies of her crew of seven into the Pacific. Of the six whose dates of birth were ascertained, each had a heavily afflicted Mars in his birth-chart, and at the time of the disaster a strong progressed aspect to Mars.

Thus is it indicated that those who contemplate following aviation as a profession, at least until it becomes less hazardous, should pay more than usual attention to the birth-chart constants and progressed constants of accidents. These are given detailed consideration, based on a statistical analysis of 100 accidents, in WHEN AND WHAT EVENTS WILL HAPPEN. Especially should those who have a powerful and afflicted birth-chart Mars, avoid hazardous journeys when there is a strong progressed aspect to Mars, particularly if the progressed aspect is discordant.

As to the ability to become an aviator, the individual should have active thought-cells such as are mapped by a prominent Neptune to attract him to flying.

To give him the required general mechanical ability, and the necessary daring, he needs also active thought-cells such as are mapped by a prominent Mars.

To enable him to handle the various electrical gadgets with which a plane is provided, and to give ingenuity in making repairs on delicate instruments, he needs active thought-cells such as are mapped by a prominent Uranus.

One who travels much must have the thought-cells mapped by the third and ninth houses unusually active. If they are not active, he will travel little; which would disqualify him as an aviator. As most aviation work involves long journeys, to attract to him such long trips, he should have active ninth house thought-cells.

The Luck Factor—Primarily he needs to have Mars, Saturn and Uranus—especially Mars, which is the chief accident planet—without such heavy discordant aspects that they indicate he will crack up.

As aviation is ruled by Neptune, any good aspect which Neptune receives is a great help, as it indicates that he will get the "breaks" that much in his favor in association with aviation activities.

Yet as most of his work also involves the ninth house, every harmonious aspect to the ruler of the ninth is a luck factor in his favor while on the journeys he must make. Aspects to the ruler of the ninth, from the luck standpoint, are probably more important than those to Neptune.

If aviators could be commanded, or persuaded, not to undertake pilot work while under progressed aspects to the planets which are the progressed constants of accidents, particularly while Mars is afflicted by progression, there would be few accidents. Even if the planets Neptune, Mars and Uranus, which give aviation ability, were powerfully afflicted in the birth-chart, accident could thus be avoided in the air. And working in a shop during such a period when by progression Mars, Saturn or Uranus was afflicted—particularly Mars—the individual would run far less hazard, and would endanger others only in a minor degree.

BOOKKEEPER

Birth-charts of bookkeepers analyzed	100	100%
Charts with Saturn prominent	100	100%
Charts with Mercury prominent	97	97%
Charts with Mars prominent	95	95%

Third House Activity of 100 Bookkeepers

Charts with third house active	94	94%
Charts with planet in third house	55	55%
Charts with third house more discordant than harmonious	55	55%
Charts with third house more harmonious than discordant	41	41%

Eighth House Activity of 100 Bookkeepers

Charts with eighth house active	91	91%
Charts with planet in eighth house	54	54%
Charts with eighth house more discordant than harmonious	52	52%
Charts with eighth house more harmonious than discordant	43	43%

In the analysis of these 100 charts by the signs occupied by the Sun, Moon and Ascendant, Libra was found to be highest—possibly because Libra dislikes dirty work and tends to neatness and precision—with twice as many as Pisces, which was lowest. Next to highest in number were Gemini and Leo, and next to the lowest were Capricorn and Aquarius. No one, however, should be disuaded from becoming a bookkeeper merely because of the sign occupied by Sun, Moon or Ascendant if the planetary prominence and house activity indicate natural aptitude for such work.

Almost invariably in these charts when the third house is weak and afflicted the eighth house is strong and well aspected; and when the eighth house is weak and afflicted the third house is strong and well aspected.

Bookkeeping or accountancy is monotonous work, in which close attention must be paid to detail. And nothing helps an individual to follow a hum-drum occupation in which there is no change or excitement, and in which precision, order and system are required, so well as active thought-cells mapped by the planet Saturn. Any work which requires a dull monotonous grind, and persistence enough not to give up until the job has been finished just right, calls upon the experiences incorporated in the Saturn thought-cells.

Any calling which requires alertness and the constant use of intelligence in solving problems, whether those problems be mechanical in nature, artistic, financial, political or mathematical, brings into expression the thought-cells mapped by Mercury. Scientists and writers are all too apt to jump to the conclusion that occupations other than their own do not require a high degree of intelligence. The intelligence which the Mercury thought-cells express, however, may find an outlet through a wide number of channels. The shrewd trader exercises the Mercury thought-cells, as does the Australian Bushman whose testimony as to the owner of any track, even though he has not seen a similar one for years, is valid in a court of law. If such a tracker has ever seen a track once, he can always identify it. And he can follow its owner in dry rock country where the white scientist cannot discern that even a pebble has been moved.

A scientist requires active Mercury thought-cells which are given a special trend by the prominence of still other planets. But if scientists think they have a monopoly on intelligence, let them try to be movie stars, waiters in a restaurant, telephone operators, or trackers through the Australian bush. They will find special training necessary even to do mediocre work in any of these vocations; and that with any amount of training they can come no nearer to doing the bushman tracker's work than with the same amount of training the bushman tracker can do theirs.

For facility with figures the mechanical qualities mapped by the Mars thought-cells are needed. We have found in teaching astrology that those with Mars lacking in prominence in their birth-charts, and with Neptune correspondingly prominent, usually are the ones who have difficulty in learning to erect a birth-chart. The same mechanical ability that enables an individual to handle other tools and to build things, seems to give ability to use arithmetic as a tool.

However, for the more abstract type of mathematics, prominent Mars thought-cells are not enough. The use of higher mathematics requires also the exercise of the Saturn thought-cells, and the more abstruse the problem, the farther removed from concrete things which can be visualized, the more the Saturn thought-cells are called upon. That is, merely to handle figures with facility requires a prominent Mercury and Mars; but to be a mathematician requires also a prominent Saturn. And to be a bookkeeper, while not requiring much mathematical ability, calls upon the Saturn thought-cells for the reason already mentioned.

While not sufficiently prominent to be considered a constant, the prominence of Uranus in the charts of bookkeepers also is sufficient to note. Uranus is the planet of short-cuts and quick methods; but its moderate prominence in the charts of bookkeepers seems to be in the nature of reinforcing the work of the Mercury thought-cells, of which the Uranus thought-cells are an upper-octave expression.

The fact that the third house in the birth-chart of bookkeepers nearly always shows so great activity undoubtedly is due to the nature of the work which is of the third house type. Writing and calculating, as well as thinking, are third house activities; and to be a bookkeeper one must thus utilize daily, and with some vigor, these third house thought-cells. And if they are to be called upon for so much work they must possess the required amount of energy.

That the eighth house commonly is quite active, although not unusually active so often as the third, seems to be due to the circumstance that the work done relates to other people's money, which is ruled by the eighth house. We find that to be strongly associated with the things of some one of the twelve departments of life, the individual must have active thought-cells mapped by the house of his birth-chart ruling that department of life.

The Luck Factor—Although Saturn is more often prominent than Mercury, bookkeeping is typically a third house and Mercury association. It would seem even more typically third house than Mercury; for Mercury thought-cell activity expresses through so wide a variety of channels. Therefore, of primary importance in appraising the general luck attracted in this vocation should be considered the aspects of the ruler of the third house. Even so, it is usually more discordant than harmonious. But it is well for it to receive at least one strong harmonious aspect, so that all the "breaks" will not be adverse. In addition, but of secondary importance, the power and aspects of Mercury should be taken into consideration.

Yet probably of as much significance in relation to luck as the third house, is the planet ruling the kind of business for which the bookkeeping is done. And as this is optional with the one seeking employment, it deserves every bookkeeper's close attention. If Mars is harmonious, bookkeeping for a hardware or manufacturing firm would prove more fortunate; if Jupiter is harmonious, a merchandising firm is indicated; if Venus is harmonious, bookkeeping where women's apparel or art objects are handled; if Uranus is harmonious, working for an automobile firm; if Pluto is harmonious, for those associated with radios, etc.

CHEMIST

Birth-charts of chemists analyzed	100	100%
Charts with Pluto prominent	100	100%
Charts with Saturn prominent	100	100%
Charts with Neptune prominent	99	99%
Charts with Uranus prominent	98	98%
Charts with Mars prominent	95	95%
Charts with Mercury prominent	93	93%

Sixth House Activity of 100 Chemists

Charts with sixth house active 93 93%
Charts with planet in sixth house....... .... 48 48%
Charts with sixth house more discordant than harmonious 58 58%
Charts with sixth house more harmonious than discordant 42. 42%

A tabulation of the 100 charts according to signs occupied by Sun, Moon and Ascendant gave Leo highest, with Virgo and Libra having almost as many. Taurus was lowest with a little over half as many as Leo; and Gemini and Cancer were next lowest.

Chemistry relates to changing the inside factors of compounds, of manipulating groups (Pluto) of atoms so that they separate from, or combine with, other atoms to form other molecules. These atoms form the inside of molecules, and Pluto rules the inside of things. The forces which cause atoms to combine into compounds relate to the fields which accompany the smallest particles of matter, invisible forces such as Pluto rules, To understand how these forces within the molecules operate, and to handle them successfully, seems to require active Pluto thought-cells. And it appears also that Pluto is the chief ruler of chemistry, and therefore of chemists. To be attracted to this calling requires active Pluto thought-cells.

The manipulation of chemicals is work of the most exacting kind. A single drop more of some ingredient than the specified amount may bring disaster. No guess work can be tolerated; everything must be measured or weighed with the utmost precision. And such precision demands that the Saturn thought-cells be active.

The chemist also must be a man of system and order. He cannot afford to hurry in his work. Instead, he must be deliberate and persistent. Without active Saturn thought-cells adequate system for handling chemicals, many of which are dangerous, is lacking.

Some of the chemicals which the chemist must handle are ruled by Neptune. Neptune not only rules gases, but is general ruler of poisons of all kinds. If the individual does not have active Neptune thought-cells it is unlikely he will be brought as closely into contact with poisons as a chemist habitually is.

Uranus is the research planet, and the thought-cells it maps in the birth-chart give the ability to discover the facts about things. And they give originality, such as a chemist must have in his analytical work. Furthermore, Uranus rules the various complicated gadgets which a chemist is called upon to use, and at times even invent, in following his work.

A chemist not only must be able to invent apparatus to meet his special needs, but he is called upon to construct many things in the laboratory. He must be a person of considerable manufacturing skill, able to make what he needs from the crude materials which he finds at hand. For such constructive ability the Mars thought-cells must be active.

As to become a chemist requires a keen mind and hard study, and its practice calls upon the intelligence constantly, he should also have the thought-cells mapped by Mercury quite active. It is not a trade to be followed by a person of dull intellect.

Chemicals, and drugs in particular, come under the rule of the sixth house. Therefore, unless the individual has active sixth house thought-cells, it is unlikely he will be sufficiently attracted into association with chemicals to become successful as a chemist.

The chemist's profession, as such, makes little call upon the social functions. It is work done in the laboratory, and depends little upon how much or how little the public likes the chemist. But when the chemist becomes a druggist, who in addition to filling prescriptions must sell to the public almost as many items as does a department store, he needs those thought-cells active in his chart which enable him to make a favorable impression on people.

If he has the Moon prominent and not too badly afflicted, it will enable him to handle the common people successfully. Even if the Moon is prominent and afflicted, he will contact many people, which has its advantages, but many of them will not like him.

A prominent Venus will enable him to give an impression of pleasantness which customers will like. This will help him draw trade. But for getting plenty of patronage there is nothing so good as active thought-cells mapped by a prominent Jupiter. People then will think him jolly, and will go far out of their way to trade with him, instead of trading with a rival.

The Luck Factor—Primarily the fortune attracted in association with chemistry in general is indicated by the aspects of the planet Pluto. But in relation to the fortune of such an association the ruler of the sixth house is only a little less important. If the vocation is to be that of a druggist, the aspects to the sixth house ruler are even more significant than the aspects to Pluto.

Chemistry, however, is practiced amid quite a variety of

surroundings. Some chemists are employed in association with mining, in which case the aspects of Saturn and the ruler of the fourth become significant. Chemists are employed where processing and dying cotton fabric is done. Under these associations the aspects to Venus are highly important as indicating the fortune attracted. Other chemists are employed where iron and steel are manufactured. And amid such association the luck would largely be indicated by the aspects of Mars.

In relation to these environments, a harmonious aspect of Pluto, which rules chemistry, to the planet ruling the association, is quite favorable. As more often than not the sixth house is more discordant than harmonious, afflictions to the ruler of the sixth should be no deterrent, provided there is at least one strong harmonious, or several weak harmonious, aspects also to the ruler of the sixth.

COSMETICIAN

Birth-charts of cosmeticians analyzed	100	100%
Charts with Neptune or Pluto prominent	100	100%
Charts with Mars prominent	99	99%
Charts with Venus prominent	93	93%
Charts with Moon prominent	90	90%
Charts with Pluto prominent	90	90%
Charts with Neptune prominent	88	88%

In a tabulation of these 100 charts by the signs occupied by Sun, Moon and Ascendant, we found that Aquarius was the highest, with Libra and Virgo next. Aries was lowest, with Cancer, Capricorn and Sagittarius next. The lowest signs had just about half as many as the highest signs. We were unable to pick any special house the activity of which conspicuously contributed to the success of these cosmeticians.

A successful cosmetician constructs something. To give a permanent, a facial massage, manicure the finger nails and give them the right polish, or any other of the numerous things a beauty operator does, requires mechanical skill, the use of tools, and some physical activity. Ability to do these things, as well as the creative impulse to build something better on the foundation at hand, and the skill to do so, whether that which is built is an airplane, an improvement to a house, or a better appearing complexion, requires that the thought-cells mapped by the planet Mars shall be active.

A cosmetician should have some artistic taste. And the refinement of feeling, and appreciation of color combinations and form, are conferred by the thought-cells mapped by the planet

Venus. That is, to be more than skilled in the use of the implements of the trade, and thus really to attain harmonious results, the artistic abilities mapped by a prominent Venus in the birth-chart should be present.

For ability to deal with the people in general, the great mass of mankind, instead of some restricted class of it, there is needed the activity of the thought-cells mapped by the Moon. Whether it be the corner grocer who sells edibles, the druggist who sells almost everything in addition to drugs, or the cosmetician who serves the desire for beauty, if there is to be contact with a large number of the common people, it is advantageous to have a prominent birth-chart Moon. Individuals without the Moon thus prominent may understand the viewpoint and tastes of those following some certain occupation or profession, but they fail to grasp the likes and dislikes of the common people, and thus are less successful in their dealing with them.

Where co-operation is essential, or a group of people work together, it is advantageous to have active Pluto thought-cells. Pluto, as the higher-octave of the Moon, signifies the spirit that should actuate a home broadened to embrace society as a whole, or some section of it, as if it were part of a larger family over which there was exercised a paternal or maternal care. It is an asset in beauty parlor work, as well as in nursing, for the operator to have such a personal solicitude for the welfare of the one being served. And those with Pluto prominent in their birth-charts can acquire this beneficial attitude.

Neptune, while not so frequently prominent in the charts of cosmeticians, is a valuable asset when present. The thought-cells which it maps in the unconscious mind are those which express as dramatic talent. And it is a function of a cosmetician to assist the client to dramatize the best points in the appearance, and to subdue and make unnoticeable the points of detraction. And those with Neptune prominent in their birth-charts have just the kind of imagination which enables them to perceive, before they actually work on a client, the effect which will be produced by a particular change, and its essential value in bringing out the result desired.

The Luck Factor—A cosmetician, no less than a physician and surgeon, is a builder, and thus must have a prominent birth-chart Mars. But as the desired result of the work has to do with beauty, rather than with strength and energy, the planet Venus is the most important single luck factor. If Venus is prominent and well aspected the luck attracted in any kind of work where beauty and harmony are outstanding in general should be good.

And those who meet the common people, whether as cosmeticians or in some retail trade, find it an asset from the luck standpoint to have the Moon harmoniously aspected.

As a third factor, not only in this work, but where the individual serves the public, the seventh house is important. An afflicted seventh house indicates there will be difficulties with customers. A well aspected seventh house tends to attract customers who are pleased with the service they receive.

DANCER

Birth-charts of professional dancers analyzed	100	100%
Charts with Venus prominent	100	100%
Charts with Moon prominent	99	99%
Charts with Neptune prominent	99	99%
Charts with Mars prominent	98	98%
Charts with Mercury prominent	97	97%
Charts with Pluto prominent	92	92%

First House Activity of 100 Professional Dancers

Charts with first house active	97	97%
Charts with planet in first house	62	62%
Charts with first house more discordant than harmonious	61	61%
Charts with first house more harmonious than discordant	39	39%

Fifth House Activity of 100 Professional Dancers

Charts with fifth house active	88	88%
Charts with planet in fifth house	52	52%
Charts with fifth house more discordant than harmonious	50	50%
Charts with fifth house more harmonious than discordant	50	50%

A tabulation of the 100 charts according to the signs occupied by Sun, Moon and Ascendant gave Leo and Virgo highest, with Gemini lowest. Gemini, Sagittarius, Aries and Cancer were low, but had more than two thirds as many as Leo, Virgo and Aquarius, which were the three highest.

Venus is the planet of harmony and grace. Dancing is a type of artistic expression, and for success in any type of artistic expression the thought-cells mapped by Venus in the chart of birth must be active. Venus also is natural ruler of partnership; and while many dances do not require a partner, many of them also do. Dancing in general is closely associated with affection for someone of the opposite sex. In other words, it is hard to imagine one becoming a professional dancer who does not have a strong love nature.

Dancing is artistic expression in which rhythm is an essential element. Venus rules harmony, but the Moon rules time and tune and the sense of rhythm. Jungle folk, who have no ear for the harmonies of a symphony, often have this sense of rhythm highly developed. They dance to the beating of tom-toms, or to a stick struck against a hollowed out stump. Often primitive people, especially the blacks, can learn and carry, or even improvise, a melody; and the melody, as apart from harmony, is ruled by the Moon. Those with active Moon thought-cells often need take no thought about learning even intricate rhythms; for their unconscious minds instantly are impressed by it, and readily deliver it to objective consciousness.

Yet a professional dancer must not only have a sense of rhythm; but he must be able to dramatize his work. The appeal to the more subtle emotions is prompted by Neptune. Whether in writing, in the business world, or other form of art, only those with active Neptune thought-cells can successfully dramatize their work. After all, professional dancing is a form of acting, and requires the active Neptune thought-cells that make for any success upon screen or stage.

But dancing makes a greater call upon muscular strength and agility than most other forms of artistic expression. It taxes the muscles even as those of an athlete are taxed. The calls upon the muscles in professional dancing are too strenuous for a person who does not have Mars sufficiently prominent in his chart of birth. Active Mars thought-cells facilitate acquiring the muscular control and skill required, and furnish the necessary creative energy. Dancing is essentially an expression of the reproductive urge; and for success in it, as in other creative art, the hormone of the gonad glands must be ample to provide a surplus of creative energy. This condition usually is present when Venus and Mars both are outstanding in the chart of birth.

Not only must a professional dancer possess the alertness conferred by active Mercury thought-cells, but he must have an exceptionally good memory. Long and intricate routines must be so thoroughly memorized that each little movement always occurs in just the right place. Many an aspirant to dancing on the stage, who had no difficulty in handling the various movements, has had to give it up because he could not quickly memorize the long routines. Such memorizing calls for active Mercury thought-cells.

Dancing of a professional nature often is done in groups. And to attract an individual to such groups, and enable him successfully to co-operate in the group activity, he needs active Pluto thought-cells. In connection with such group activity one at once thinks of the work of chorus girls.

Where personality enters prominently into the work the first house, which rules it, is important. People with weak first house thought-cells seldom are able to capitalize on their personalities. But a dancer greatly depends upon his stage personality, the grace and beauty of his body in particular, in his work. Therefore it is highly important that he should have an active first house. The table indicates that quite a high percentage of professional dancers have first house thought-cells that are more discordant than harmonious. However, these discords are probably seldom manifest on the stage; they are discords that enter into their personal contacts with other dancers and other people which are chiefly discernible in their conduct and relations when not actually entertaining the public. But a dancer should have first house thought-cells active enough to give a vigorous stage personality.

As professional dancing is work which has to do with entertaining, it means fifth house associations during all the time the profession is followed. Therefore, to attract these associations the fifth house thought-cells should be active.

The Luck Factor—As dancing is ruled by Venus, the fortune that is likely to be attracted in association with this profession is largely denoted by the aspects of Venus. If Venus is too badly afflicted, difficulties will constantly be cropping up. Yet if Venus has one powerful harmonious aspect, and the planets which give natural aptitude for this work are outstanding, the individual may make a pronounced success of dancing in spite of the difficulties.

Important from the luck standpoint, but not so important as Venus, are the harmony and discord of the fifth house thought-cells as indicated by the aspects to the ruler of the fifth. Of those who actually follow dancing as a career the table shows that half of them have the fifth house thought-cells more discordant than harmonious. Therefore, if there is ability, and Venus has one strong harmonious aspect, the individual need not feel discouraged in reference to this calling; especially if the fifth house thought-cells are quite active, as indicated by its ruler being prominent in the chart.

DENTIST

Birth-charts of dentists analyzed.	100	100%
Charts with Jupiter prominent	100	100%
Charts with Mercury prominent.	100	100%
Charts with Saturn prominent	99	99%
Charts with Mars prominent	98	98%
Charts with Venus prominent	98	98%

Sixth House Activity of 100 Dentists

Charts with sixth house active.	97	97%
Charts with planet in sixth house	44	44%
Charts with sixth house more discordant than harmonious	58	58%
Charts with sixth house more harmonious than discordant	37	37%

A tabulation of the 100 charts according to the signs occupied by Sun, Moon and Ascendant gave Aries and Virgo highest, and Sagittarius lowest with a little more than half as many. Next to the highest was Leo, and next to lowest were Gemini and Cancer.

Those who are not contented merely to follow a trade, or merely to work with their hands, but have the feeling of abundance strong enough that they follow a profession, have active Jupiter thought-cells. Active Jupiter thought-cells tend to cause the individual to feel that life holds something better for him than a manual occupation. They work also to attract to the individual the opportunity to prepare himself for some profession; for law, medicine, the clergy, dentistry, or even the best type of astrologer; or to get him into salesmanship work or merchandising. But a person who does not have Jupiter prominent in his chart of birth has the utmost difficulty in getting into a profession.

Jupiter is the planet of good-will and geniality which are so important in attracting patronage. The Jupiter thought-cells thus not only work to cause the individual to take up a profession, but they give the warmth and geniality which cause people to like him and come to him for service.

To become a dentist requires study and alertness, which are seldom possible to those who do not have active Mercury thought-cells. But there also is another reason Mercury thought-cells must be active in those who follow dentistry. Upon the Mercury thought-cells must depend the degree of dexterity; and few occupations require finer manipulations with the hands than does dentistry. If the dentist bungles the merest bit, the patient instantly suffers, and probably goes to another dentist.

Saturn rules the teeth, and to draw one into close association with them Saturn should be prominent in the chart of birth. But there again we have a second, and perhaps even more important reason for the prominence of the planet. A Jupiter-Mars individual who had sluggish Saturn thought-cells, when confronted with a decaying tooth would be for jerking it out. Just as a certain type of doctor seems satisfied only when removing an appendix or some other part of the anatomy. But a dentist's chief job is to save teeth, to make them last as long as possible.

He exercises the greatest ingenuity in making repairs so that the tooth may be saved and not removed. This is typically Saturn work.

Not only the structure with which he works, the teeth, and the effort to save them as long as possible, but also the painstaking care with detail, and the slow laborious work with minute cavities, are typical of Saturn. I believe, therefore, we are safe in saying that dentistry is mainly a Saturn occupation. And to be a good dentist the Saturn thought-cells should be active.

It is also work requiring mechanical skill, and the building of something, and therefore needs active Mars thought-cells. Even not to mind the pain others suffer, providing it is for their own good, also requires active Mars thought-cells. Neither Mars nor Saturn conduce to sensitivity. Both are harsh, and do not too greatly mind the suffering of others. And a dentist should not be hypersensitive.

The doctor with Jupiter prominent can radiate warmth, geniality, and a confident optimism which encourages his patient and gives people confidence in his skill. But the dentist needs something not necessary for a doctor. He needs to keep people entertained while he drills their teeth and hammers repair material into cavities. He wants to take their mind off what he is doing as much as possible, and this he does, if he is competent, through interesting conversation.

A dentist does not need to be a good mixer out of office hours; but if he is to keep his patients coming back he should be a social fellow who apparently is interested in their affairs. That is one reason he needs active Venus thought-cells. The other is that on these thought-cells he must depend for good taste and artistic appreciation; and it is his job to give people teeth that are artistic and pleasing to behold. Artificial teeth must be not merely good looking in themselves, but they must be in proper taste for the individual who wears them.

The ailments of people, including the difficulties they have with their teeth, come under the rule of the sixth house. The dentist depends on people with sick teeth for his livlihood. And unless he has active sixth house thought-cells he is not sufficiently attracted to people who are in some manner ailing to get patronage. Thus a dentist as well as a doctor or a nurse should have an active sixth house.

The Luck Factor—Primarily as the success he has with teeth determines his prosperity, at least in so far as his patients give him advertising, the luck he will attract in associating with them is primarily indicated by the aspects of Saturn, which rules teeth. If Saturn should be in good aspect to the Moon, or the Moon the best planet in the chart, it indicates success with women patients. If it is in good aspect with Mercury, or if Mercury is the best planet in the chart, the success would be outstanding with children. If Mars were in good aspect to Saturn, or were the best planet in the chart, the dentist would do well to take up practice in a neighborhood where mechanics live. If Neptune were the best planet in the chart, or even if it were in good aspect to Saturn, he might do better in a locality where moving picture patronage could be contacted. Or if Jupiter were a good planet, or harmoniously aspecting Saturn, instead of working to build up trade among the common people, he could with advantage establish himself where it would be possible to contact professional people, or people of some wealth.

Of secondary importance as a luck factor is the sixth house. If the sixth house is badly afflicted, the patients he gets will be difficult cases, and he will have many obstacles to overcome. Yet the table shows that much more than half of the dentists analyzed had a sixth house more discordant than harmonious. Therefore if the ruler of the sixth has at least one strong harmonious aspect, or several weak harmonious aspects, even if badly afflicted otherwise, there would be no serious deterrent to taking up dentistry.

There is another factor, not analyzed in the table, but of considerable importance in following any of the professions. It is the harmony or discord of the seventh house thought-cells. We have not analyzed it because if the natural aptitudes for dentistry are strong, and Saturn and the sixth house have some harmony, an afflicted seventh house should not stand in the way of following this profession. And it would cause difficulty in any profession, or any calling that depends upon close contact with patients or clients.

A harmonious seventh house indicates thought-cell activity that tends to cause those served to be satisfied with the work done. But an afflicted seventh house attracts those who are apt to be dissatisfied with the services no matter how good those services may be. Clients or patients of a person who has a heavily afflicted seventh house are inclined to be troublesome. And the nature of their troublesomeness is indicated by the ruler of the seventh and the planets afflicting it.

DOCTOR

Birth-charts of doctors analyzed	100	100%
Charts with Mars prominent	99	99%
Charts with Jupiter prominent	99	99%

Sixth House Activity of 100 Doctors

Charts with sixth house active	99	99%
Charts with planet in sixth house	45	45%
Charts with sixth house more discordant than harmonious	51	51%
Charts with sixth house more harmonious than discordant	47	47%

Twelfth House Activity of 100 Doctors

Charts with twelfth house active	99	99%
Charts with planet in twelfth house	99	99%
Charts with twelfth house more discordant than harmonious	58	58%
Charts with twelfth house more harmonious than discordant	39	39%

We tabulated the signs in which the Sun, Moon and Ascendant were located in these charts of 100 doctors; but no sign stood out with sufficient prominence to warrant special mention.

The June, 1937, issue of AMERICAN ASTROLOGY MAGAZINE gives the result of tabulating the Sun-signs of 7,000 physicians, as compared with a prominence normal, which in turn was based upon the birth-dates of 66,000 prominent persons. This gives Capricorn as high, with 9.75% above the normal, and Sagittarius as low, with 10.48% below the normal. Rather surprisingly, Scorpio, which usually has been considered the physician's sign, is next lowest, with 10.15% below normal.

Running through a number of issues of AMERICAN ASTROLOGY MAGAZINE during 1936, there were Sun-sign analyses of the charts of 6,877 physicians. They were variously grouped according to their specialty, and in addition to the sign of the Sun, the Sun-decanates also were tabulated, and the sign in which Mars was found.

While there was a variation from the average, much as is shown above in relation to the prominence normal, in none of these different analyses did any sign appear low enough that it would warrant discouraging a person born with the Sun in the sign from endeavoring to become a physician; nor did any sign appear sufficiently high to constitute it a birth-chart constant.

In the matter of Mars being prominent in the birth-chart, however, it stands out so conspicuously in the 100 doctors' charts we analyzed, that it would seem folly for any person not having this planet prominent in his birth-chart to attempt healing as his profession. Building and tearing down are activities typical of the Mars thought-cells. And only those who have these Mars thought-cells sufficiently active are capable of making a success of an occupation calling for either destructive or constructive ability.

In addition to the skill in surgery, in the administration of medicine, and in other methods of repairing the body, which active Mars thought-cells give; the mental and personal atmosphere of the physician, through their power of suggestion, are very important factors in the work of healing. A prominent Jupiter in the birth-chart maps though-cells which give warmth, geniality, and a confidant and optimistic attitude which are communicated to the patient.

It is not merely what the healer says to the patient; but those most successful, as a rule, have a bearing and a personal atmosphere which gives the patient confidence that the doctor will be able to affect a cure.

Furthermore, it is difficult for those who do not have quite active Jupiter thought-cells to get into any profession. A prominent Jupiter not only causes the individual to feel that life holds something better for him than a manual occupation; but the work of the thought-cells so mapped tends to attract to the individual the opportunity to prepare himself for a profession, or to get into salesmanship work or merchandising.

Jupiter is the planet of that good-will and geniality which attract patronage. The thought-cells mapped by a prominent Jupiter, therefore, not only help the individual to get into professional work, but give the assurance that people will like him well enough, and have sufficient confidence in him, that they will employ his services.

Among the doctors whose charts we have analyzed have been a number of chiropractors. These, and those who depend much upon electrical devices and high-frequency rays, have Uranus conspicuously prominent in their charts of birth. Uranus also seems to favor new and unusual methods.

Those who rely upon Naturopathic treatments, Stellar Healing, Massage and similar drugless methods of healing, commonly have Neptune conspicuously prominent in their charts of birth; as do those who give Metaphysical, New Thought, Divine, Spiritual and other forms of absent treatments.

People who continuously are brought in contact with sickness must have unusually active thought-cells occupying the sixth compartment of their astral bodies. This does not imply that a planet must actually occupy the sixth house; but that, at least, the planet ruling the cusp of the sixth must receive powerful aspects.

While only a portion of the doctors are associated with hospitals, yet the sick-rooms which they constantly visit are frequently places of confinement and restriction to the patient; sufficiently so to come under the influence of the twelfth house. At least, the thought-cells related to the twelfth house in the charts of doctors we have analyzed show outstanding activity.

So far as Natural Aptitude is concerned, one who intends to become a doctor should have within his unconscious mind thought-cells such as are mapped by a prominent Mars, a prominent Jupiter, an active sixth house and an active twelfth house.

The Luck Factor—In the matter of so-called luck, it is better, though not essential, to have Mars and Jupiter each receiving at least one harmonious aspect. Mars is the ruler of the healing profession, and its aspects have some significance in reference to the harmony or discord attracted in such work.

The luck which will be attracted in association with the illness of people is indicated by the harmony or discord of the ruler of the sixth house; and the luck which will be attracted in association with hospitals or rooms of confinement is indicated by the harmony or discord of the ruler of the twelfth house.

There are those who follow the healing profession who have only discordant aspects to the rulers of the sixth and twelfth, but these are at a great disadvantage. Skill must be exceptional to overcome the handicap of the continuous difficulties thus attracted; and those who are outstanding in the healing profession have at least one powerful harmonious aspect, along with discordant ones, to the ruler of the sixth and to the ruler of the twelfth.

DRAFTSMAN

Birth-charts of draftsmen analyzed	100	100%
Charts with Mercury prominent	100	100%
Charts with Neptune or Venus prominent	100	100%
Charts with Mars prominent	97	97%
Charts with Venus prominent	91	91%
Charts with Neptune prominent	88	88%

Third House Activity of 100 Draftsmen

Charts with third house active	100	100%
Charts with planet in third house	58	58%
Charts with third house more discordant than harmonious	70	70%
Charts with third house more harmonious than discordant	30	30%

A tabulation of the signs in which the Sun, Moon and Ascendant are found reveals there are more draftsmen in Leo and Cancer, with almost as many in Libra and Pisces; while Aries,

Taurus and Sagittarius contain fewest, with only about two-thirds as many as in the four favored signs. Yet as many successful draftsmen are born under Aries, Taurus and Sagittarius, this does not warrant discouraging a person from taking up the vocation simply because he is born under a strong influence from one or all of these three signs.

Drafting is a form of mental expression requiring dexterity, alertness, and clear-cut objective thinking such as active Mercury thought-cells alone can afford. Mercury rules the nerve currents; and if there is to be fine co-ordination between the images in the mind and muscular action, there must be sufficient brain-cell activity and nervous control, such as is present only among those who have Mercury prominent in their birth-charts.

The muscles are ruled by Mars, and skill in their use, such as a draftsman must employ, requires that the Aggressive thought-cells in the astral body shall be more than commonly active. Moreover, most draftsmanship is employed in the precise plotting of something for the purpose of gaining more ready knowledge of it, or in plans or designs from which something is to be built. This implies a knowledge of mechanics or of structural work which is easily acquired only by those who have the Aggressive thought-cells active, as indicated by a prominent birth-chart Mars.

Successful drafting requires that the sheets when finished shall be neat and attractive in appearance. Proper lettering is often an important feature. The artistic appearance essential to success in this work is chiefly made possible through the activity of the Venus thought-cells. However, even when the Venus thought-cells are not so active, if those mapped by its upper-octave, Neptune, are quite active, the work does not suffer in appearance. Thus we can say that either Venus or Neptune, and better, both, should be prominent in the chart of one who expects to follow drafting as a calling.

Drafting, like writing, is a third house activity; and if one is to do sufficient work to make a success of this occupation, he must have enough activity on the part of the thought-cells mapped by the third house to attract it. Those who do drafting, who do much writing, or who study consistently, not merely while going to school, but after leaving it, must have third house thought-cells activity of the kind which is mapped by the ruler of the house powerfully aspected.

The Luck Factor—Like writing and teaching, drafting seems to come under the general rulership of Mercury. And like these two other Mercury occupations, it is carried out amid a wide variety of associations; permitting considerable choice, which can be utilized in the selection of the luck factors.

It is, of course, better from the luck standpoint if Mercury has at least one good aspect, though this is not essential to becoming a successful draftsman. When afflicted, Mercury tends to attract difficulty through little errors and oversights, not only upon the part of the person in whose chart it is thus afflicted, but upon the part of others. Thus to prevent misfortune in an occupation ruled by Mercury, an individual with this planet heavily afflicted in his birth-chart, and particularly when it is also afflicted by a progressed aspect, must take unusual care to check against little errors on his part, and to take precaution that the errors of others do not cause serious difficulty.

Of secondary importance from the luck standpoint is the harmony of the thought-cells of the third house. 70% of the charts analyzed had the third house more discordant than harmonious; but if the ruler of the third house receives at least one strong harmonious aspect, or several weak harmonious aspects, success will be more assured. The more harmonious the aspects made to the ruler of the third the better the luck attracted in this, or other, third house occupation.

But even when Mercury and the third house are severely afflicted, if the thought-cells mapped by them are active enough to give marked natural aptitude for this work, it often is possible to select a field in which to utilize the drafting talent that will attract considerable luck.

Drafting is employed in map making of all kinds relative to real estate, and in mining and the development of natural resources and basic utilities. To the extent the planet Saturn is harmonious in the birth-chart would good fortune tend to be attracted in employing drafting or other talents in connection with such matters, or in the work of an architect.

In designing and installing machinery, and in tool making, draftsmanship plays an important part. The luck that could be expected to be attracted through such associations is indicated in the birth-chart by the amount of harmony or discord shown by the planet Mars. That is, if the Mars thought-cells in the astral body are pronouncedly discordant, any continuous association with machinery or sharp tools would greatly increase the tendency to accident and strife. On the other hand, if the Mars thought-cells are harmonious, the association with tools and machinery gives them additional energy and opportunity to work from the inner plane to attract fortunate events into the life.

The luck that would be attracted in association with aviation, air-conditioning and the movies is largely indicated by the aspects made to Neptune in the birth-chart. In association with radio work, or television, it would be determined by the aspects to the planet Pluto.

Draftsmanship, or other occupation, in which there is constant work relating to electricity, would be influenced in the luck factor by the aspects made to the planet Uranus. That is, even mental association with things electrical adds energy to the Uranus thought-cells within the astral body, which enables them to do more work from the inner plane. And the fortune or misfortune of the events attracted through this inner-plane work is chiefly determined by the harmony or discord of these Uranus thought-cells.

ELECTRICIAN

Birth-charts of electricians analyzed	100	100%
Charts with Uranus prominent	100	100%
Charts with Pluto prominent	100	100%
Charts with Mercury prominent	98	98%
Charts with Mars prominent	97	97%
Charts with Mars aspecting Uranus	71	71%

In the analysis of these 100 charts by the signs occupied by the Sun, Moon and Ascendant, Libra and Sagittarius were found to be highest, and Taurus, Gemini and Pisces lowest with not quite two-thirds as many. Next to the highest were Virgo and Scorpio, with Aries and Cancer trailing closely. Aquarius, even though ruled by Uranus, the planet of electricity, had only two more than Pisces and three more than Taurus and Gemini.

In addition to the specific abilities conferred by Uranus, as this planet is the ruler of electricity, only those who have it prominent in their charts of birth seem strongly enough attracted to things of an electrical nature to make close association with them a portion of their daily lives. For instance, if you will turn to the analysis of telephone operators you will find that Uranus was prominent in nearly all the charts of those analyzed who follow that vocation. And it is stated that the prominence of Uranus in those charts probably had little to do with the magnetic power of this planet to influence others, but more likely related to the association between the planet and gadgets, such as the switchboard affords, and to electricity, which Uranus rules; which are essential parts of a telephone system.

This is even more true as applied to electricians, because magnetic personalities seem even less essential to them than to telephone operators, because the variety of gadgets they handle is much greater, and because the association with electricity is even more intimate.

Yet instead of catering to a wide public, such as is ruled by the Moon, and keeping it pleased and comfortable, the electrician is called upon to exercise constant ingenuity in repairing, installing, and adjusting a vast assortment of gadgets ranging in size from huge generators and dynamos down to minute and delicate instruments. Thus the inventive ability which is distinctive of Uranus is called into play in the everyday work of an electrician more pronouncedly than in most vocations.

The prominence of the planet Pluto in the charts of electricians evidently does not relate to this planet's rulership over group activity of people, but to its significance where hidden forces and the inside of things are concerned. Pluto is the planet of inner-plane forces, and of intra-atomic energies. To determine precisely where the domain of Uranus ends and that of Pluto begins will require painstaking research, but the evidence to date indicates that the influence of one somewhat overlaps and blends into the influence of the other.

Thus it seems that electricity and electromagnetic fields under the more ordinarily observed conditions are ruled strictly by Uranus. But when an alternating current is given so high a frequency that the electromagnetic fields produced by the moving electric impulses do not fold back, but become electromagnetic waves, such as those used in radio, the energy then seems to come under the domain of Pluto. Of course, the transformation of one kind of energy into another kind having a different planetary rulership is not unusual, for mechanical (Mars) energy can be used in the generation of electriciy. But in such conversion the line of demarcation is rather clear.

The electromagnetic radiations of the energies generated in man's nervous system may, in various degrees, be converted into the high-velocity energy of the inner plane. Because the two planes can exchange motions only through such electromagnetic forces, we call them Boundary-Line energies; and after the conversion from Boundary-Line energies to inner-plane energies is complete we consider them then ruled by Pluto.

Yet Pluto, as well as Neptune and Uranus and some of the other planets, also has rulership over certain electromagnetic radiations which may convert some of their energies into those of the inner plane. That is, Pluto not only rules inner-plane energies, but also certain of the Boundary-Line electromagnetic energies which, still possessing a velocity not greater than light, readily can communicate their motions to substance having higher-than-light velocity. As Pluto has a higher side and a lower side which are quite distinct, I believe we are warranted in concluding that it rules not only inner-plane energies, but the Boundary-Line energies which most readily contact them.

The electrician is not called upon to understand anything about inner-plane energies, but his work does require that he become familiar with unseen electromagnetic forces and visualize how they act. He is not required to measure cosmic rays, which to penetrate the electromagnetic field surrounding the earth at Mahur, India, must possess 17 billion electron volts, according to Dr. Millikan. But he must be able to ascertain the probable current generated in a telephone wire one hundred feet distant, for instance, from a high-tension power line carrying a given number of volts. And while neither the telephone wire nor the electricity carried by the power line are ruled by Pluto, it does seem that Pluto prominent in an electrician's chart facilitates his grasp of how unseen forces, including those electromagnetic, operate at a distance.

The prominence of Mercury indicates that only those with considrable intellectual ability are suited to become electricians.

The prominence of Mars relates to the mechanical ability that must be employed. The Mars-Uranus aspect being so prominent indicates that mechanical ingenuity is at a premium among those who become electricians. Mars is the mechanical and constructive planet, and Uranus is the planet of ingenuity. Uranus aspecting other planets tends to give ingenuity relative to the matters these other planets rule. Thus its aspect to Mars favors ingenuity relating to mechanics and building things.

The Luck Factor—As electricity is ruled by Uranus, we must judge the luck factor chiefly from the aspects to this planet. This does not mean that a chart with heavy afflictions to Uranus cannot succeed if Uranus also has some help. George Westinghouse, for instance, organizer of the great Westinghouse Electric Company, had Uranus in the fourth house opposition Mars, Mercury and the Sun. But he had it also trine Jupiter in the seventh house, which always, from his youth on, enabled him to contact wealthy (Jupiter) partners (seventh) who would finance his ventures, even after he had had disastrous business difficulties. And Thomas A. Edison had Uranus semi-square Sun and square Moon; but he also had it sextile Jupiter and trine the M.C. He went bankrupt on occasions, but his reputation

(M.C.) as an inventor (Uranus) and his ability to contact people of wealth (Jupiter) enabled him to go ahead again after each reverse. In other words, both of these men had many misfortunes arising out of electricity, but each had such outstanding ability that they needed only an occasional "lucky break," as signified by the mentioned harmonious aspects to Uranus, to attain outstanding success.

ENGINEER

Birth-charts of engineers (electrical, civil, mechanical, construction, aviation, radio, etc.) analyzed	100	100%
Charts with Uranus prominent.	100	100%
Charts with Mars prominent	100	100%
Charts with Saturn prominent	100	100%

Tabulating the signs in which Sun, Moon and Ascendant are found, Leo in these 100 charts runs about 30% above average, Libra, Scorpio and Cancer about 10% above average, and Pisces about 30% below the average. Yet no one should be discouraged from taking up engineering merely because the Pisces influence in his chart is outstanding; for engineers with such positions are not uncommon, as this analysis shows.

The suggestion has been put forward in various quarters that an aspect from Mars to Uranus gives engineering ability. Yet this certainly can not be considered a birth-chart constant of engineering, as in 47 of these charts no such aspect was present.

Almost any type of engineering requires ingenuity and the ability to solve problems. Such ability is present to the extent the Individualistic thought-cells are active, as mapped by a prominent Uranus.

Engineering more commonly is employed in association with constructing something. The natural aptitude for any type of creative endeavor or building is largely measured by the amount of activity of the Aggressive thought-cells within the unconscious mind, mapped by the planet Mars. Only those with a prominent birth-chart Mars should engage in creative work, or in engineering.

To become a successful engineer, an individual must be prepared to shoulder responsibility, and to work hard and persistently. He must have system and foresight, be able to reason logically, and to make successful plans. Only those who have the thought-cells active such as are mapped by a prominent birth-chart Saturn, possess such qualifications.

The Luck Factor—Granted that an individual has Uranus, Mars and Saturn all quite prominent in his chart of birth, and and thus has natural aptitude for becoming an engineer, he will do well to look carefully to the luck factor. And as in engineering there is a wide variety of associations with which the work can be performed, one preparing to enter this field usually has ample opportunity to select conditions such as will attract much misfortune or considerable luck.

The luck attracted, in each instance, is determined by the planetary ruler of the things with which the engineer is chiefly concerned. In so far, for instance, as there is association with machines, the thought-cells mapped by Mars are involved; and even in those types of engineering work which are not primarily concerned with engines, such as mining engineering, structural engineering, electrical engineering, etc., machines frequently play an important part.

In addition to aviation engineering, which increasingly makes calls for outstanding talent, there is now some demand for engineers who are familiar with air-conditioning, for those who can handle certain problems in connection with the motion picture industry, and for others who are sufficiently familiar with the oil industry. These associations all are ruled by the planet Neptune, and if this is a prominent and well-aspected planet in the birth-chart, it indicates the fortune would be better in one of these fields.

As a field for the engineer who has a prominent and well-aspected Pluto, there is at present radio engineering; while the future holds forth the promise of television and the transmission of power by electromagnetic waves. The force of the cosmic ray, and that which holds the electrons and atoms together, as yet are merely the subjects of experiment. But when the time arrives when such invisible forces are utilized commercially, the engineer with a powerful and well-aspected Pluto in his chart will be the one most fortunate in association with them. As chemistry also is ruled by Pluto, the luck attracted in association with chemical engineering is chiefly to be appraised from the aspects to this planet.

To the extent the thought-cells mapped by Uranus are active and harmonious, is luck apt to be attracted in association either with electricity or with intricate gadgets and new mechanical inventions. For the special ability to understand electricity and handle it, look to the prominence of Uranus in the birth-chart. But for the luck or misfortune apt to be attracted in following the profession of electrical engineer, look to the aspects which the planet Uranus receives.

Civil engineering and those types in which land, timber, or other natural resources are chiefly involved, bring the things ruled by Saturn to the fore. If the thought-cells mapped in the birth-chart by Saturn are discordant, such association will bring an almost unceasing train of difficulties. But if Saturn is well-aspected, this type of work will bring advantages and opportunity for advancement. In the development of irrigation projects, or flood control and soil erosion hindrances, the Saturn associations would be typical.

The engineering work associated with the development of hydro-electric power, would bring in a luck factor ruled by Saturn, and also another luck factor, that mapped by Uranus, in reference to the electricity.

Mining engineering, while the mining part proper, and the removal of coal or ore from the ground, has a luck factor ruled by Saturn, also commonly involves to a somewhat less degree a Mars luck factor, because of the constant use of machinery; and a Uranus luck factor due to the use of electricity as a source of power in modern mining operations.

The luck factor in mechanical engineering is clearly that of Mars. To the extent the Aggressive thought-cells mapped by this planet in the birth-chart are harmonious will good fortune be attracted in the use of tools, machines and engines; and to the extent these thought-cells are discordant is there a tendency to accident and other types of misfortune in such use.

Structural engineering has a luck factor ruled by Mars. This represents the constructive activity, the use of machines and tools, and the structural iron work. Yet it also has a Saturn luck factor. The concrete commonly used in association with structural iron, and the building itself, are ruled by Saturn.

Such charts as we have of those who have made a success of building city skyscrapers, have both a prominent Mars and a prominent Saturn. In one instance, while exceptionally prominent, they were terribly afflicted. Yet this individual had a fine seventh house, and made a fortune while in partnership with another man. He had charge of the engineering and building part of the work, and permitted his partner to have exclusive charge of the financial part. As soon as the partnership broke up, which it eventually did, he commenced to lose money and have misfortune. This is mentioned to indicate the manner in which one man, with exceptional ability for structural engineering, overcame for many years, the afflictions of Mars and Saturn in his chart of birth.

FARMER

Birth-charts of farmers analyzed	100	100%
Charts with Saturn prominent	100	100%
Charts with Pluto or the Moon prominent	100	100%
Charts with Pluto prominent	92	92%
Charts with Moon prominent	88	88%

Fourth House Activity of 100 Farmers

Charts with fourth house active	100	100%
Charts with ruler of fourth member of heaviest configuration in chart	87	87%
Charts with planet in fourth house	49	49%
Charts with fourth house more discordant than harmonious	58	58%
Charts with fourth house more harmonious than discordant	40	40%

The tabulation of the signs in which the Sun, Moon and Ascendant were found in these 100 charts brought out some quite unexpetced data. For instance, it has generally been held that farmers were more apt to be those with these influences in earthy signs; yet in 45 of these charts the Sun, Moon and Ascendant were in other than earthy signs; which shows the earthy well below average.

Curiously enough, and also contrary to prevalent opinion, not only Virgo but Libra ran highest, with 40% above average. Perhaps the fact that Libra is the exaltation of Saturn, the farmer planet, has something to do with its high rating; yet the signs ruled and co-ruled by Saturn, Capricorn and Aquarius, ran low. Virgo, the harvest sign, running high was in conformity with prevalent opinion.

Aquarius ran lowest, with 24% below average, and Taurus, Scorpio and Capricorn next lowest, with 12% below average. Yet Taurus has commonly been considered a farming sign, and Libra a sign avoiding agriculture.

Saturn has always been considered the planet of farmers, and was prominent in all of these charts. It is an occupation in which the labor is hard and monotonous and the hours of work long. In the past, at least, it has meant giving up some of the conveniences of city life, a lack of which is typically Saturn.

The farmer, to be successful, must have both patience and planning ability, which only those possess in the required degree who have the thought-cells active in their unconscious minds such as are mapped by a prominent Saturn. The farmer must plan to plant his crop at the most favorable time, and take into consideration probable prices he will receive for various products, and when they will be ready for market. His income, instead of being a rather continuous supply, comes merely at those intervals when his stock or his produce is fit for market. Many farmers are dependent upon a crop that is harvested only at one time; and they must wait twelve months between sales, and so systematically plan their expenditures that the income received at one time must last a year. Only those with active Saturn thought-cells have the patience and foresight to make a success of such a life.

The Moon is the general ruler of nutrition; and the farmer supplies the food of the world. Quite commonly, in addition to crops raised directly from the soil, the farmer depends also in some degree upon raising animals large or small. Perhaps even the looking after the grain in the fields, and taking pains it gets a fair start, and is not choked out by weeds, consists of looking after the weak and helpless. At any rate, raising chickens and live stock of the larger kinds requires a certain amount of mothering capacity. And such capacity, as is clearly indicated in the charts of nurses, depends upon the activity of the Domestic thought-cells, ruled by the Moon.

Pluto is the planet of universal welfare and of mass production. It is the upper-octave expression of the Moon's influence. In the looking after the young and helpless of both plants and animals there is in some degree the universal welfare attitude. But more particularly is a farmer's work associated with mass production; mass production of fruits and grains and vegetables and stock. Thus we find that farmers have the thought-cells mapped by Pluto quite prominent, and I believe we are warranted in discouraging any person from taking up farming who has neither Moon nor Pluto prominent in his chart, or whose chart lacks a prominent Saturn.

However, as quite a number of people with Sun, Moon or Ascendant in Aquarius succeed in farming, even though this is the least numerous of the signs which follow this occupation, I do not think we are warranted in discouraging Aquarian people, or those born under any other sign, merely on that account, from taking up farming.

People who do not have active fourth-house thought-cells do not have persistent association with the land. Their thought-cell activities attract them to some different environment, which is ruled by the house of their charts mapping active thought-cells. That is, they become associated with writing, with journeys, with entertainment, with business, or whatever in their charts is represented by a house of outstanding activity.

As farming requires incessant contact with the land, any

person who does not have the ruler of the fourth house powerfully aspected is unsuited to it.

The Luck Factor—As Saturn is the ruler of farmers, the aspects in the birth-chart to Saturn are significant of the luck that would be attracted while following this occupation.

But of at least as much importance, and perhaps more, in reference to the luck factor, are the aspects received by the ruler of the fourth house. If there is no harmonious aspect to the ruler of the fourth, the luck attracted while associated with the land will be rather uniformly bad. Yet, as the table shows, it is not necessary to have the fourth house ruler receiving nothing but good aspects to have sufficient luck in this occupation to do fairly well.

Handling live stock of the larger kinds, especially where range riding is involved, has a strong element of Mars; and for such work the Mars thought-cells must be considered in determining the luck factor. But in general, the luck with large animals is to be determined from the ruler of the twelfth house; and the luck with small animals, such as rabbits, chickens and pigs, from the ruler of the sixth house.

LAWYER

Birth-charts of lawyers analyzed	100	100%
Charts with Mercury or Uranus prominent	100	100%
Charts with Saturn prominent	99	99%
Charts with Mercury prominent	96	96%
Charts with Uranus prominent	95	95%
Charts with Jupiter prominent	89	89%

Ninth House Activity of 100 Lawyers

Charts with ninth house active	100	100%
Charts with planet in ninth house	53	53%
Charts with ninth house more discordant than harmonious	59	59%
Charts with ninth house more harmonious than discordant	40	40%

An analysis of the signs occupied by the Sun, Moon and Ascendant in these 100 charts gives the lead to Leo, Libra, Sagittarius and Capricorn; with Gemini and Pisces taking low places. The difference between the high and the low, however, is not significant enough to point to any sign as a birth-chart constant of lawyers. Nor is it important enough that people with Sun, Moon or Ascendant in Pisces or Gemini should be discouraged from taking up law, provided the indicated planets are prominent and the ninth house is sufficiently active.

As the practice of law so commonly involves a contest, we also tabulated the activity of the seventh house; but in these 100 charts its ruler receives aspects little, if any, stronger than that of the average of charts. The activity of the ninth house, however, stands out even more significantly than it does in the charts of writers.

Uranus is the upper-octave of Mercury. Both of these planets have a direct influence over the nerve currents and the processes of thinking in terms of words and sentences. A lawyer requires an active mind, alertness, shrewdness, the ability to study, and facility in expressing himself. In all these charts of lawyers, as mapping thought-cells whose activities give these qualifications, either Mercury or Uranus is prominent. To the extent Mercury, in any lawyer's chart is lacking in prominence, Uranus is unusually prominent; and to the extent Uranus is somewhat lacking in prominence, Mercury *is* unusually prominent.

The ability to work hard at monotonous work, to systematize evidence, and to reason logically are mapped by the planet Saturn. The thought-cells thus signified must be active for logical reasoning, for foresight, for ability to map out and plan a campaign, and to devise successful schemes for trapping the opposition. That is, the drudgery and painstaking toil of preparing a brief, finding flaws in evidence, and planning the method to be used in legal matters requires active Saturn thought-cells.

To present such evidence convincingly to a jury, however, requires a very different group of thought-cells. To read human nature correctly, and through oratory to sway the minds of others, requires active thought-cells of the Uranus type. Upon such thought-cells also must depend such brilliance as is used in questioning witnesses, or in devising unusual methods to win the desired result.

For patronage in any of the professions, as well as in selling more tangible goods, the good fellowship of the Jupiter thought-cells must largely be dependent upon. Jupiter gets the work to do because people like the individual who has the thought-cells it maps prominent. Yet, as indicated by 11% of these lawyers not having the Jupiter thought-cells unusually active, an individual can make a success of law, if he has enough ability otherwise, with very little help from the thought-cells of good will. That is, even if people do not care for him, if he gets a reputation for winning cases, he will get their patronage. Also, he may do valuable work in a law firm, without much direct contact with patronage.

Not infrequently, a partnership in which a lawyer strongly Mercury-Saturn in type is joined to one of the Uranus-Jupiter type proves quite successful. The Mercury-Saturn individual is an authority on business law, and on legal matters in general. He lays the plans, works up the cases, and looks after details. The Jupiter-Uranus member of the firm meets people, attracts business to the firm, and when a case is in court, does the pleading before the judge or jury.

Jupiter prominent in a chart assists the individual to acquire a profession. But when Jupiter is not prominent, a prominent Sun may enable him to become a lawyer, as it did in eleven of these charts; for when Jupiter was not prominent the Sun was.

It seems, in addition to the prominence of the planets indicated, that it would be unwise to encourage any person, the thought-cells in whose astral body mapped by the ninth house were not more than normally active, to enter the profession of law. Association with the courts is attracted by the thought-cells mapped in the ninth section of the astral form. If these thought-cells are not unusually active there will be little association with legal matters, and therefore little success in connection with them.

The Luck Factor—Uranus, probably more than any other planet, is the ruler of lawyers. From the luck standpoint, therefore, it is better to have at least one strong and harmonious aspect to Uranus. This will give favorable "breaks" in the contacts with other people often enough to prevent the obstacles to be overcome being too consistently difficult.

But as the court, the judge and the jury are ruled by the ninth house, it is probably even more important from the luck standpoint, that all the aspects to the ruler of the ninth house should not be discordant ones. If all are discordant, whenever the matter of favor comes up, there will be a tendency on the part of the court or the jury to decide against the lawyer.

On the other hand, as shown by 59 of the charts having stronger discordant aspects to the ruler of the ninth than harmonious ones, it is not essential that the ninth house thought-cells be predominantly harmonious. The more active they are, the more important such matters will be. And if, at the same time, he can be assured of getting the "breaks" in his favor even part of the time, and his ability is outstanding, as shown by the prominence of the lawyer planets, he should be able to make quite a success. Outstanding personages in the legal profession nearly always have at least one powerful harmonious aspect to the ruler of the ninth.

If Jupiter is particularly harmonious in the chart, he could specialize in law for merchants or professional men. If Saturn were exceptionally well aspected in his chart, he would have the luck factor in his favor if he became an insurance lawyer, or looked after the legal interests of miners or real estate men.

With good aspects to Venus his legal practice might be given a luck turn through specializing in affectional matters; a divorce lawyer, for instance, if the seventh house also showed outstanding activity. Or if the Sun were well aspected in his chart, he could direct his efforts toward getting the patronage of politicians, or executives. With good aspects to Mars or Pluto, he could become a criminal lawyer.

In law, as in most other matters, if an individual has sufficient ability, it is possible for him to gain success in spite of persistent unlucky occurences. But if he can associate with something, in the practice of his profession, which tends to attract luck to him, he can attain a higher success, and more surely, and with less struggle.

MACHINIST

Birth-charts of machinists analyzed	100	100%
Charts with Mars prominent	99	99%
Charts with Saturn prominent	98	98%
Charts with Uranus prominent	96	96%
Charts with Mercury prominent	95	95%

In a tabulation of these 100 charts by the signs occupied by Sun, Moon and Ascendant, we found that Libra was highest with 32% above the average, Scorpio next highest, and then Leo. The lowest sign was Capricorn, with 36% below average. Taurus was next lowest, and then Pisces. No sign was conspicuous enough, however, to be considered a constant, and none low enough that a person should be discouraged from becoming a machinist merely because of the prominence of some sign. We were not able to pick out any special house whose activity was significant in the charts of machinists.

It takes the ability conferred by the thought-cells mapped in the unconscious mind by Mars to handle tools skillfully. And it takes the energy thus mapped to give the desire to build something or to destroy something; and the more Mars energy is present the greater the desire to express through some constructive or destructive channel.

The energy mapped by a prominent Mars, even when the planet is greatly afflicted, can be diverted into constructive work of some kind. And if it is not thus put to constructive work, we may be sure it will find an outlet in some destructive activity. The gangster who beats up those who do not bow to his dictates, who robs a bank at the point of a gun, or who holds up pedestrians on the highway is expressing Mars energy in a way that is inimical to society, and which probably will bring the loss of his freedom if not of his life, because that Mars energy was not conditioned earlier in life to find a satisfactory expression in something constructive.

Those who have youngsters in charge accept a grave responsibility, and especially so when one of their charges has a powerful and greatly afflicted birth-chart Mars. In such a case it is imperative that an outlet be found for the Mars energy which is not detrimental to others, but trains at least indirectly for some useful creative work, and which gives the youth a feeling of pride and relieves the creative drive in a feeling of satisfaction. We have much reason to believe that any youth of normal intelligence, taken early enough, and handled correctly, instead of becoming a hoodlum or bandit, no matter how powerful and afflicted Mars may be in his chart, can be made to take pride in being a useful citizen. But only through encouraging, and not repressing, the expression of the creative energies, and diverting them through appeals to whatever other urges may be powerful, into constructive channels that give them satisfaction.

Mars energy can express through any type of creative work, and is required for creative art or creative intellectual effort. And even to brain workers, it gives a facility in the use of tools if they devote any time to handling them. But when Saturn and Uranus also are prominent the creative ability expresses with facility through mechanical lines.

Saturn inclines to laborious types of work, even when they are purely mental. And when prominent it gives the persistence to undergo the apprenticeship or other training necessary properly to learn a trade. A machinist is called upon to do heavy labor. The machines on which he works are ruled by Mars, as are the tools which he uses. There is nothing soft, yielding, or of the Venus nature about his work. It has the harshness and the concreteness of Mars and Saturn. And to learn the trade the individual must apply himself persistently over a period of years.

While Mars gives activity and skill, it is the thought-cells mapped by Saturn that demand care and the utmost in precision. Mars alone is inclined to work rapidly, and to employ dexterity. But the painstaking attention to detail which makes a competent machinist is conferred by the energies mapped by a prominent Saturn. And Saturn also enables the machinist to lay his work and plan its details in advance, so that each operation shall be performed in the order that will give the greatest advantage.

A workman in the assembly line of an automobile plant may have Uranus prominent in his birth-chart; but if his duty requires only that he tighten a certain nut, or some other operation that he does over and over endlessly, he is not using the Uranus thought-cells, and they are apt to cause great restlessness. Instead, he is using the thought-cells of Mars and Saturn; and the more routine the job is, and the more monotonous, the greater his need for active thought-cells such as are mapped by Saturn to hold him to his job. One with Saturn lacking in prominence develops nervous disorders if a job is too monotonous.

But in the ordinary work of a machinist there are ever new problems that require solving. And while Mercury must be prominent enough to give intelligence, and a certain amount of alertness, the ingenuity to invent some new way of doing something, or of making a repair, or of handling some new mechanical situation, requires that the thought-cells mapped by Uranus shall be prominent.

The heavier types of routine work requires only a prominent Saturn and Mars, but the more delicate types of work, which especially require the use of new gadgets or their repair, require also a prominent Uranus. And if the work is connected with electrical devices, or with automobiles, which are ruled by Uranus, the need for this planet's influence is all the greater.

As in the work of a machinist the handling of figures plays a part, and precise measurements must be made, the Intellectual thought-cells mapped by Mercury should be sufficiently active. In other words, while a machinist is not required to take a classical education, nevertheless, in his mechanical education there are innumerable things he must learn and not forget, and to do his work he should not be mentally dull.

The Luck Factor—The luck that may be expected while following this vocation is chiefly to be determined from the aspects of Mars, which rules both the work and its associations. As automobiles are ruled by Uranus, Uranus well aspected in the chart, and particularly if there is a favorable aspect from Mars to Uranus, indicates good luck in association with automobiles. And as Neptune rules aircraft, to the extent Neptune is well aspected will associating with them prove fortunate.

The aspects of Mars itself, however, mainly determine the luck to be expected in association with tools and machinery in general. Yet Uranus and Saturn cannot be entirely ignored; for in the matter of accident, while not nearly so significant as Mars, they also some of the time play a part. That is, if the accident planets—Mars, Saturn and Uranus—are too heavily afflicted, the individual should avoid, as much as possible, situations where accidents readily happen. In that case, instead of actually working with tools or in a machine shop, the individual may be able to capitalize on his natural mechanical aptitudes through demonstrating a machine, through selling machinery, or through some other avenue, as indicated by a harmonious planet in his chart, where the hazard of injury is considerably less.

MOVIE ACTOR

Birth-charts of movie stars analyzed	100	100%
Charts with Mars prominent	98	98%
Charts with Uranus prominent	94	94%
Charts with Neptune prominent	89	89%
Charts with Mercury prominent	79	79%
Charts with Venus prominent	74	74%

Fifth House Activity of 100 Movie Stars

Charts with fifth house active	93	93%
Charts with planet in fifth house	58	58%
Charts with fifth house more discordant than harmonious	43	43%
Charts with fifth house more harmonious than discordant	53	53%

First House Activity of 100 Movie Stars

Charts with first house active	91	91%
Charts with planet in first house	54	54%
Charts with first house more discordant than harmonious	58	58%
Charts with first house more harmonious than discordant	40	40%

We tabulated the signs in which the Sun, Moon and Ascendant were located in these charts of 100 movie stars; but no sign stood out with sufficient prominence to be significant, and certainly not sufficiently to be a birth-chart constant of movie actors.

Something more than mere beauty is required to get into pictures; in fact, a glance at the photographs of the leading movie picture stars is convincing that beauty of the classical type is not a requisite. That which all of them do have, however, is personality. Either on the stage or on the screen, those most successful have a personality which grips and holds the attention of the audience.

Such a personality must be energetic. It must have either the force or the vivacity which is the outward expression of unusually active thought-cells of the type mapped by Mars. And if it is to fascinate, and hold others by a spell which is something more than ordinary charm, the thought-cells mapped by Uranus also must be unusually active.

Because the name of those who aspire to a movie career is multitude, and because the salary of such as reach eminence in the profession is enormous, it is one of the most highly competitive of all vocations. And to meet this competition, to fight to get proper recognition, to prevent those of less talent but of more aggression from shoving the actor to one side, there must be present the combative qualities mapped by a prominent birth-chart Mars.

Mars is the planet of creative energy, and to the extent an art is creative, must the thought-cells mapped by Mars be active. Furthermore, contrary to public opinion, when movie actors work, often it is during long hours and under great pressure. Over limited periods of time, great drains are made upon their energies, and they must be able to withstand fatigue, the criticism of directors and associates, and other difficulties which would discourage any but those of a fighting spirit. Such is the significance of Mars prominent in the birth-charts of 98% of the movie stars.

An actor's task is not merely to feel the part he is playing, and portray it accurately. To be successful, he must make others intensely feel as he does; he must be able to sway them emotionally. And nothing gives the individual so much power to influence the minds and conduct of others as do the thought-cells mapped by the planet Uranus. Even though no electromagnetic radiations emanate from the actor on the screen, the audience instantly, through some subtle sympathy, recognizes, and responds to, the screen portrayal of a magnetic personality.

Merely a cut and dried rendering of the action and the words of the script, never promoted an actor to stardom. He must have the originality to devise a better method of portraying the part given him. Ever must he be on the alert to find new methods by which to improve his work. This necessity for ingeniousness and the ability to handle portrayals in new and better ways, is shown by Uranus, the planet of originality, being prominent in 94% of the movie star charts.

Uranus, as is commonly recognized, is also the most unconventional of all the ten planets, and the most disruptive to domestic relations. Its prominence in the charts of movie people, together with the prominence of Neptune, which not content with imperfection, ever seeks the ideal, no doubt accounts for the number of divorces among screen celebrities, and the great publicity attached to them.

The activity of the thought-cells thus mapped also accounts for the well known fact that nearly all movie people are interested in astrology and some form of occultism. When the thought-cells mapped by Uranus are active enough to quite dominate those mapped by the other planets, they enable the actor to devise eccentric or unusually original parts. Such parts, for instance, as those played by Charlie Chaplin and Harold Lloyd, both of whom have Sun opposition Uranus.

Whether that ability be used in promoting some business, in getting recognition for one's personality, in the rendition of a musical symphony, in the portrayal of characters in fiction, or upon the movie set, the measure of an individual's dramatic ability is the prominence of Neptune in his chart of birth. There are those who have attained to movie stardom, through special fitness for certain parts, or who have other natural aptitudes of outstanding merit, yet who have little real dramatic talent. But when the thought-cells mapped by Neptune are quite active, it gives facility to submerge the personality in widely different roles. Gloria Swanson, for instance, has it in opposition to her Ascendant, and Geraldine Farrar, who made a success as a prima dona, as well as on the screen, has it conjunction her Ascendant.

It often has appeared in print that movie actors are unintelligent. In fact, one author terms Hollywood a colony of morons. But when we find that Mercury is prominent in the charts of 79% of the stars analyzed, we can not agree with such a view. On the contrary, these are the charts of exceptionally quick-witted people, who may, or may not, be versed in the classics; but who undoubtedly possess far more than the average ability to adapt themselves successfully to new situations.

When the Intellectual thought-cells are unusually active, as shown by Mercury exceptionally prominent in the chart, they may cause the individual in his screen work to assume the role of a clever character. This was the case with Johnny Fox, the tough kid in The Covered Wagon, who has Mercury in the tenth house. And although the thought-cells mapped by Uranus in her seventh house are responsible for the eccentricity of the characters she portrays, the Intellectual thought-cells also manifest clearly in the work of Louise Fazenda, who has Mercury on the cusp of her fourth.

In addition to the prominence of Mars, Uranus, Neptune and Mercury; Venus, the planet of grace and beauty is also prominent in 74% of the movie star charts. Some of the movie talent, particularly those who play comics or take the villain parts, are far from being either graceful or beautiful. But when the thought-cells which receive energy from this planet are unusually active, as is the case when Venus is exceptionally prominent in the birth-chart, it not only lends grace and beauty, but it attracts the actor to roles in which grace of manner combines with meticulousness of dress. Such roles have been portrayed by Rudolph Valentino, Adolph Menjou, Bert Lytell and Rod La Roque, all of whom have an unusually prominent Venus.

The Luck Factor—In addition to the prominence of the five-mentioned planets, it is a great asset, especially if these planets, as often is the case, are heavily afflicted, to have a powerful and well aspected fifth house. Neptune is the planet having general rule over the moving picture industry and acting. And its aspects thus have some significance in reference to the luck attracted in association with these industries.

But more specifically, the fifth house of a birth-chart rules entertainment, including that of stage and screen. Therefore, if the thought-cells contained in this fifth section of the unconscious mind are active and harmonious; whenever there is association with stage, screen or other type of entertainment, it affords these thought-cells opportunity, working from the inner plane, to attract good luck into the lift.

Perhaps because the competition is so strenuous, those who climb to the top in movie acting seem to have more need of the luck furnished by harmonious aspects to the house relating to their profession than do those engaged in other callings. This does not mean there must be a planet well aspected in the fifth house, but that the ruler of the fifth needs at least some favorable aspects. For instance, Norma Shearer, who has been starring in pictures for years and years, has no planet in the fifth; but Uranus, ruler of its cusp, is member of a grand trine.

In addition to the "lucky breaks" in moving picture work which a good Neptune, or of more importance, a powerful and harmonious fifth house attracts, it should be noted that the type of character portrayed is strongly influenced by the most powerful trend in the birth-chart.

Wm. S. Hart, the two-gun man, who often portrayed the part of a criminal bad man, dealing death to all and sundry, has Mars the most elevated planet in his chart, in the house of death (eighth) in square to Sun, Mercury, Venus and Saturn in the twelfth (house of crime). In the chart of Douglas Fairbanks, Sr.,

Mars in Aries is the most elevated planet, sextile Mercury, and trine Moon in Sagittarius, the sign of sports and athletics. Athletic stunts, chivalry, and sportsmanship marked his work. Roscoe Arbuckle, with Mars conjunction both Sun and Moon in Aries in the tenth, while doing comedian work (as Aries, more than other signs tends to do), gave it a distinctly Mars turn in its roughness and Wild West setting.

MUSICIAN

Birth-charts of instrumental musicians analyzed	100	100%
Charts with Moon or Neptune prominent	100	100%
Charts with Mars prominent	88	88%
Charts with Saturn prominent	86	86%
Charts with Moon prominent	86	86%
Charts with Neptune prominent	82	82%
Charts with Venus prominent	79	79%

Fifth House Activity of 100 Instrumental Musicians

Charts with fifth house active	100	100%
Charts with planet in fifth house	41	41%
Charts with fifth house more discordant than harmonious	51	51%
Charts with fifth house more harmonious than discordant	49	49%

In a tabulation of these 100 charts of instrumental musicians by the signs occupied by Sun, Moon and Ascendant, we found that Virgo, Aquarius and Pisces were highest, with Leo next. Taurus was lowest with more than half as many as Virgo, and Capricorn was next lowest. No sign stands out as significant of ability as an instrumental musician.

Vocal Musician

Charts of vocal musicians analyzed	25	100%
Charts with Moon or Neptune prominent	25	100%
Charts with Mars prominent	24	96%
Charts with Moon prominent	21	84%
Charts with Neptune prominent	19	76%
Charts with Saturn prominent	17	68%
Charts with Venus prominent	16	64%

In tabulating these 25 charts of vocal musicians by the signs occupied by Sun, Moon and Ascendant, we found Leo the highest, with Sagittarius a poor second. Much the lowest was Capricorn, with Aries and Pisces next lowest. Too much reliance can not be placed on this factor, however, due to the fact we were able to get only 25 timed birth-charts.

Composer of Music

Birth-charts of composers analyzed	25	100%
Charts with Uranus or Neptune prominent	25	100%
Charts with Uranus prominent	24	96%
Charts with Neptune prominent	23	92%

Musical Conductor

Birth-charts of musical conductors analyzed	10	100%
Charts with Uranus prominent	9	90%
Charts with Mars unusually prominent	9	90%

While Venus is the planet of art, lending beauty and harmony to its expression, high artistic performance in any of its forms requires a surplus of creative energy, such as is given by the thought-cells mapped by Mars prominent in the birth-chart. Music, in nature, is chiefly the expression of the reproductive urge, ruled by Mars. Birds, for instance, more commonly sing only in courtship and during the time they are mated. Thus also, according to these tables, human musicians, to be successful, need unusually active Mars thought-cells.

Furthermore, as the Aggressive thought-cells rule the muscles, these, when Mars is prominent, facilitate acquiring the muscular control and skill which is so essential either to instrumental or vocal performance.

To become a musician requires plodding perseverance; and this aptitude for hard work and long hours of monotonous practice is conferred by the Safety thought-cells; which accounts for the prominence of Saturn in musicians' charts.

Time and tune and the sense of rhythm are conferred by the Moon thought-cells. They give a natural aptitude for carrying melody. The tables do not give full justice to the Moon; for in most of the charts in which it is prominent, that prominence is exceptionally outstanding.

The Neptune thought-cells enable the musician to dramatize his work; to give it feeling. The appeal to the finer and more intricate emotions is that of Neptune. It is the ruler of cultural music, and not only those who do symphony work, but most of those who love the symphony, have Neptune prominent in their charts. Jazz is the expression of the Moon and Mars thought-cells, with little influence either from Neptune or Venus. Among vocalists whose performances were not mechanical, but attractively dramatic, Adelini Patti, Marion Talley and Lillian Russell had Neptune in the seventh house, and Geraldine Farrar had it on the cusp of her first.

The thought-cells mapped by Venus give a good ear for harmony and tone, and its aspect to the Moon or Mercury lends grace and artistry to musical expression.

Conductors need more of the Mars creative energy, and more of the ability to influence others through the personal magnetism given by a prominent Uranus. The one chart out of the ten, of directors analyzed, which has neither Uranus nor Mars prominent, is that of Louise Antonio Birco, said to be the first woman in 70 years to lead the Philharmonic Orchestra of Berlin. Unmarried, affecting masculinity in dress and actions, she has attained high musical honors. Moon is on the M.C., and leadership is shown by Sun conjunction Ascendant. Sun, Neptune and Mercury are on the Ascendant in close conjunction.

For originality, such as composers should have, Uranus must be prominent in the birth-chart, and for fine feeling and fertility of imagination, a prominent Neptune is required. All the great composers of the 25 analyzed have both Uranus and Neptune prominent in their charts.

As a result of these analysis, should a chart be brought to me to judge if some boy or girl should take up music as a profession, I should first look to the prominence of the Moon and Neptune. If neither the Moon nor Neptune were prominent, I should discourage such a course.

If the Moon were prominent, especially if in an angle; or to a lesser degree if the Moon were not prominent but Neptune were prominent, I should consider the child had some natural flair for music. This flair, however, would not lead far unless there were also the creative energy mapped by a prominent birth-chart Mars, and the persistence to keep doggedly at practice conferred by a prominent birth-chart Saturn.

The Luck Factor—For the luck attracted in association with music, as it is largely used in entertainment, look chiefly to the fifth house, giving Venus, the general ruler of music and other arts also some consideration. Madame Schumann-Heink, for instance, has two planets in her fifth, one of them Jupiter, in sextile to the Sun.

Radio broadcasting is one of the several ninth house methods of reaching the public. Even as Neptune rules moving pictures, so Pluto rules the radio. Those who have a prominent Pluto in their birth-charts are more apt to take to radio work of some kind than are others. Thus for radio work, the aspects of Pluto have some significance in reference to the luck attracted. But of more importance in radio work, so far as the luck factor is concerned, is the power and harmony of the ninth house. The luck attracted in association with the movies may be determined from the harmony of the fifth house and the aspects of Neptune.

NURSE

Birth-charts of nurses analyzed	100	100%
Charts with Moon prominent	100	100%
Charts with Mars prominent	100	100%
Charts with Pluto prominent	97	97%

Sixth House Activity of 100 Nurses

Charts with sixth house active	100	100%
Charts with planet in sixth house	53	53%
Charts with sixth house more discordant than harmonious	62	62%
Charts with sixth house more harmonious than discordant	35	35%

Twelfth House Activity of 100 Nurses

Charts with twelfth house active	95	95%
Charts with planet in twelfth house	52	52%
Charts with twelfth house more discordant than harmonious	59	59%
Charts with twelfth house more harmonious than discordant	40	40%

A tabulation of the signs in which the Sun, Moon and Ascendant were found gave no variation from normal sign distribution of sufficient importance to warrant mention; and certainly did not indicate any sign to be a birth-chart constant, or that those with some other sign prominent should be discouraged from taking up nursing.

The thought-cells within the unconscious mind which have been derived in the past from experiences in taking care of the helpless and looking after their wants, such as commonly is involved in the parenthood of various forms of life, are chiefly mapped in the birth-chart by the Moon. To the extent there have been many and intense experiences of this kind in the evolutionary past, is there a natural aptitude for looking after those weak or ill. Thus must those with ability for such work have in their birth-charts a prominent Moon.

The actual work of rebuilding the body, as well as the work of building anything else, is an activity of the Aggressive thought-cells. For any creative work the thought-cells mapped by Mars must be unusually active. And as a nurse, in the sense of one who looks after those who are ill rather than one who merely looks after the comforts of children who may be quite healthy, is expected to look after the rebuilding of the human body, he must, to be successful, have thought-cells within his astral body such as are mapped by a prominent birth-chart Mars.

Other than the prominence of the professional planet, Jupiter, in the chart of doctors, there is another difference between their charts and those of nurses. Both the doctor and the nurse must have Mars prominent, not merely because the work required is constructive in nature, but also to give the ability to witness the pain of others, and to do things unflinchingly which cause others great suffering, if it contributes in the long run to the healing process. But in the charts of professional nurses the Moon is usually more prominent than Mars, standing out quite conspicuously, and giving them a desire to minister to other people's wants; while in the charts of doctors it is not even a birth-chart constant.

There are those who take up nursing merely because it affords an opportunity to make a living. But those most successful in such work have a deep desire to serve a useful purpose in the world, and take a very real pride in being able to relieve the suffering of others. This attitude derives largely from the thought-cells in the astral body mapped by the planet Pluto, and most nurses have this universal welfare planet prominent in their birth-charts. Through its rulership of Scorpio, Pluto also may have some affinity with the destructive and constructive attributes of Mars. At least, its thought-cells make for drastic action, and a good nurse cannot be a milk and water individual.

The Luck Factor—As nursing is a vocation ruled by the Moon, the thought-cells mapped by this planet have primary luck significance to those who follow it. Nurses commonly are under instructions from doctors, and often are dependent upon their recommendation for employment. The tendency to fortune or misfortune through doctors is indicated in the birth-chart by the aspects received by Mars.

If one does not have an active sixth house, one is not brought continuously into association with illness, and therefore one does not become a nurse. The extent one will have luck or misfortune through associating with those sick, is determined by the harmony or discord of the thought-cells mapped by the sixth house, which is shown by the aspects of the ruler of the sixth.

Even when nursing is not in association with a hospital, commonly hospital experience is required in the training; and even apart from such an institution, the sick room, as a place of confinement, bears relation to the twelfth house. The luck in such associations is determined from the aspects made to the ruler of the twelfth.

It seems advisable, therefore, for one who contemplates nursing as a vocation, to have at least one strong harmonious aspect to the ruler of the sixth house; and better also to have at least one harmonious aspect to the ruler of the twelfth.

POLICEMAN

Birth-charts of Policemen analyzed	100	100%
Charts with Saturn prominent	100	100%
Charts with Mars prominent	100	100%
Charts with Pluto prominent	97	97%
Charts with Neptune prominent	95	95%

Twelfth House Activity of 100 Policemen

Charts with twelfth house active	100	100%
Charts with planet in twelfth house	51	51%
Charts with twelfth house more discordant than harmonious	57	57%
Charts with twelfth house more harmonious than discordant	40	40%

Tabulating the 100 charts according to the signs occupied by the Sun, Moon and Ascendant showed Cancer, Leo, Virgo and Libra more numerous; with about an equal number in each. The fewest had these factors in Aquarius, next fewest in Pisces, with Gemini only a little more numerous than Pisces. Yet policemen are sufficiently numerous with Sun, Moon and Ascendant in Aquarius that no one should be discouraged from taking up this vocation because these factors are in that sign. Nor can any one sign be considered the birth-chart constant of the vocation to the extent that one should be encouraged to take it up on the strength of sign positions.

The work of a policeman is mostly routine in nature. This monotonous sameness, which most of the time is present, can be endured only by individuals who have the thought-cells mapped by Saturn unusually prominent. And even those whose work lends itself to greater variety, must have Saturn thought-cell persistence of purpose to follow the criminal unrelentingly until a capture is made.

Those who are too soft hearted are unfitted for police work. Saturn is the planet of strict and unbending justice, and the thought-cells he maps, to the extent they are dominant influences in the life, encourage the attitude that those who infringe upon the rights of others should pay a commensurate penalty. There is no flexibility to Saturn, no tendency to permit humanitarian feelings to deflect the individual from that which he has accepted as his duty. There is a rigid demand that the letter of the law be enforced, and a desire to haul the misdoer before the bar of justice.

Mars in most of these charts not only was prominent, but afflicted; more often than not by the Moon, than which no aspect gives more courage and daring. Police work would be a poor occupation for any person who is timid, or who makes a special effort to avoid danger. While much of the life is dully monotonous, there are intervals in which initiative, action and a willingness to enter into personal combat with desperate men are required. Those who do not have the Aggressive thought-cells in their astral bodies sufficiently active, an activity which is mapped by the prominence of birth-chart Mars, do not enjoy work in which the possibility of deadly strife is ever before them. Only a prominent birth-chart Mars denotes one who is sufficiently willing to face physical danger to become successful as a policeman.

The underworld in general, and the criminal in particular, come under the rule of Pluto. It is a policeman's business to keep in touch with these anti-social individuals, that he may protect society from their depredations. Furthermore, he does not work against crime single-handed, but in cooperation with other officers; and this co-operative ability also is mapped in his birth-chart by the prominence of the planet Pluto.

Policemen, within the field wherein they operate, also are dictators. The traffic officer's gestures take precedence over mechanical signals; and officers in general are given authority by the group of society which they serve to enforce the law. This representing the group will, and the authority to use force in behalf of the group will is typical of Pluto; and the table indicates that those who succeed in police work have the thought-cells mapped by Pluto quite active.

But to apprehend criminals it is not sufficient alone to be daring. One must be able to scheme, and to lay traps for them. Neptune is the traditional trapper and fisherman. And it seems that those who do not have certain thought-cells in their astral bodies sufficiently active, as mapped by a prominent Neptune, are lacking in ability to catch their quarry in the proverbial net of the law. Apparently this Neptune prominence, as well as twelfth house activity, is especially important in the charts of those doing secret service work.

The Luck Factor—While the thought-cells mapped by Saturn must be prominent in the birth-charts of policemen, all law-enforcement officers, as well as soldiers, come chiefly under the rulership of Mars. And as Mars rules this vocation, its aspects have an important bearing upon the luck attracted while following it. This Mars luck factor relates chiefly to the tendency toward accident and strife while engaged in police work. That is, if Mars chiefly, and the other accident planets—Saturn and Uranus—strongly indicate a tendency toward accident, the individual in his police duties would be apt to become injured seriously in his attempts to enforce the law; particularly at those times in his life when there is a major progressed aspect to Mars within one degree of perfect. If the progressed aspect to Mars were inharmonious, the danger would be greater.

Criminals in general, and those who, as most criminals now do, have gang affiliations, are ruled by Pluto. As a policeman's duties compel him to come in close contact with such individuals, both to prevent crime and to take criminals into custody, the Pluto luck factor also should be given some consideration. If Pluto were harmoniously aspected, he would tend to be lucky in such contacts; but if Pluto were too heavily afflicted by discordant aspects, he would attract misfortune through the activities of criminals. One of the most characteristic methods by which those of the Lower-Pluto type defeat the efforts of law-enforcement officers, is either to get some actual evidence of misconduct which can be held over the officer, or to manufacture such evidence in such a way that the officer dares not discharge his duty properly for fear of consequences to himself.

Criminals are the secret enemies of society, and, like the places where they are confined when apprehended, belong to the department of life mapped in the birth-chart by the twelfth house. One who expects to become a policeman, therefore, should have not merely thought-cells mapped by Saturn, Mars, Pluto and Neptune prominent, but he should have active twelfth house thought-cells, such as are indicated by its ruler being powerfully aspected. If he does not have such a birth-chart he should be discouraged from taking up law-enforcement as a vocation.

In much the same way that the planet Pluto maps by its aspects the luck to be expected from contact with criminals, so also is the ruler of the twelfth house similarly significant. If it is discordantly aspected, it brings difficulties when there are attempts at crime detection and contact with criminals. But if the ruler of the twelfth has at least one powerful harmonious aspect, there is opportunity for sufficient luck in that department of life that the individual need not be encouraged from becoming a policeman.

Most policemen have more discordant aspects to the ruler of the twelfth than harmonious ones, and most of them experience a commensurate amount of poor luck. Yet as only 6 out of the 100 analyzed had nothing but discordant aspects to the ruler of the twelfth, unless there is at least one harmonious aspect to this twelfth house ruler, the obstacles to be overcome in making a success of police work are so great that it seems wiser for the individual to direct his energies into some other channel.

POLITICIAN

Birth-charts of politicians analyzed	100	100%
Charts with Sun prominent	100	100%
Charts with Pluto prominent	97	97%
Charts with Uranus prominent	97	97%
Charts with Mercury prominent	86	86%
Charts with Jupiter prominent	84	84%

Tenth House Activity of 100 Politicians

Charts with tenth house active	100	100%
Charts with planet in tenth house	64	64%
Charts with tenth house more discordant than harmonious	54	54%
Charts with tenth house more harmonious than discordant	44	44%

We also tabulated the activity of the seventh house, but in these 100 politicians' charts, it showed no activity above or below normal. The signs in which the Sun, Moon and Ascendant were located in these 100 charts were tabulated; but none was found sufficiently important or unimportant to warrant special mention; and certainly none can be considered as a birth-chart constant of politicians.

The drive for significance is the most ancient and deep seated of all the motives of life. Without the thought-cells mapped by the Sun, which have been built in the past through experiences with significance, sufficiently active and harmonious, there is no incentive to carry on, and the organism lacks vitality and recuperative power. These Power thought-cells also are the chief source of an individual's ability to win the obedience of others.

The ability to exercise authority is dependent upon the intensity and volume of the activity of these thought-cells mapped in the birth-chart by the Sun. This is true not merely in politics, which because it implies leadership and the exercise of authority is ruled by the Sun; but in all walks of life. The shop foreman or the department store floorwalker, to the extent others take orders from him and are obedient to his requests, must have active thought-cells such as are mapped in his birth-chart by a prominent Sun.

The vocation of a politician is that of directing the activities of other men. Whether he gains a position of authority through election or appointment, or exercises his power without general public consent as a precinct boss, he must have the sense of leadership and the power to dominate others which alone unusually active Sun thought-cells can give.

Pluto is the general ruler of dictators, and the dictator type of politician needs active Pluto thought-cells. But even if not given to dictating, anyone who handles groups of people needs these thought-cells active; and ability to handle people in groups, or in large masses, is highly advantageous to anyone who aspires to political honors.

Even more important probably, and next in importance to the sense of significance conferred by the Sun and its power to impress others, the politician, to be successful, should have the high voltage magnetism by which, either in personal contact, or through oratory, he can sway the minds of others. Active Sun thought-cells give a volume and persistence in the generation of electrical energies which enables the individual to exercise considerable control over himself and over others. The personal magnetism thus developed gives others a feeling of reliability and solid strength.

But the electric energies generated by the activity of the Uranus thought-cells, while unstable and erratic, have a much higher voltage. And if these thought-cells are unusually active, as mapped by a prominent birth-chart Uranus, the personal magnetism is powerful enough quite to overcome the electricity generated by the nervous system of others, and exercise a dominating force. These shorter wave-length radiations of Uranus sweep others off their feet and cause them to sponsor political programs, and become wildly enthusiastic over ideas, which if submitted to calm Saturnine reason, they would be quick to reject. To be able to enthuse others and influence their minds, the politician must have the thought-cells active which are mapped by the planet Uranus.

A politician needs to be shrewd. Always there are others who strive to take his position from him, or who, for their own selfish purposes are willing to cast discredit upon him. A slow witted person, or one unable quickly to adjust himself to new situations, is easily defeated by his rivals. Furthermore, one who purposes to lead others, and to exercise authority, should be a person of ideas. Thus he should have active Intellectual thought-cells, such as are mapped in his birth-chart by a prominent Mercury.

All have encountered the hand-shaking type of politician, the person who tries never to forget a name (a Mercury prominent accomplishment), and who greets each individual he meets as a cherished friend. This type usually goes to great pains, also, to do favors for people. And because he is so well liked, rather than because he is competent, people vote for him, or those he has granted favors bring pressure to bear in the right places to insure an appointment.

This good will factor, and the joviality and fellowship which result either in patronage or votes, is an expression of the Religious thought-cells. To the extent these thought-cells are active, does an individual have ability of this kind. And the more prominent Jupiter is in his birth-chart, the more active are these good will thought-cells thus mapped.

Politics is essentially a tenth house association in two different ways. The tenth house maps the thought-cells which relate to public office and to the administration of any business, private or public. Therefore, if one is to be consistently and closely associated with the administration of the business of the people, one must have tenth house thought-cells active enough to attract such association.

But in addition to this, political preferment, even when the exercise of political power is not known to the public at large, largely depends upon reputation, which in turn relates to the thought-cells mapped by the tenth house. Even the grafting ward heeler, if he is to retain power among those whose voting he directs, must retain the faith of his lieutenants that they will be rewarded as he promises. Whatever his reputation may be where the outside public is concerned, he must retain the reputation of always rewarding those who work for his interests with commensurate favors. Thus is it essential for one who takes up politics as a vocation to have an active tenth house.

The Luck Factor—In politics there are ways of utilizing various luck factors. Inharmonious aspects to the Sun indicate Power thought-cells that will attract difficulties in the exercise of authority. It is fortunate, but not essential to political success, to have the Sun receiving at least one strong harmonious aspect. Such an aspect tends to attract favors from those in authority, as well as helping in the harmonious administration of it.

As political power is so dependent upon reputation, which is mapped by the tenth house, it is a good luck indicator in this vocation to have a well aspected M.C. or a well aspected ruler of the tenth house. Yet our table shows that while all politicians had active tenth house thought-cells, that 54% of them had aspects to the ruler of the tenth more discordant than harmonious; although only 5% had nothing but discordant aspects to the ruler of this house of reputation.

When the birth-chart constants of the vocation are present, some politicians, in spite of Sun and tenth house afflictions, are able to go a long way through utilizing the luck factor of an active and harmonious house of friends (eleventh). They cultivate friendship on every hand, and whenever possible avoid making enemies, and depend upon these friends to bring sufficient pressure to bear to give them the desired office in spite of reputation and difficulty in exercising authority.

There have been those who have used the luck factor of a harmonious second house, through contributing to political campaigns and charitable and public enterprises, to assist them politically. Yet when the tenth house is too greatly afflicted, and with no harmonious aspect to the M.C. or the ruler of the tenth, it seems wiser not to aspire to a position obtained through popular election; although a well aspected Moon is a luck factor of much value in winning such a popular contest. Instead, the politician should seek an appointment office, or push someone else to the front, on whom he can depend to carry out the sound policies he originates.

RADIO TECHNICIAN

Birth-charts of Radio Technicians analyzed	100	100%
Charts with Pluto prominent	100	100%
Charts with Uranus prominent	100	100%
Charts with Mars prominent	100	100%
Charts with Mercury or Moon prominent	100	100%

Ninth House Activity of 100 Radio Technicians

Charts with ninth house active	95	95%
Charts with planet in ninth house	43	43%
Charts with ninth house more discordant than harmonious	56	56%
Charts with ninth house more harmonious than discordant	43	43%

A tabulation of the 100 charts according to sign occupied by Sun, Moon and Ascendant gave Libra highest, with Virgo, Taurus and Gemini next highest. Sagittarius was lowest with two fifths as many as Libra, and Aries next to lowest with only one more than Sagittarius. Thus there would be no basis for either encouraging or discouraging any person from becoming a radio technician merely because of the sign Sun, Moon, Ascendant or planets were in.

Electromagnetic waves not only are used to transmit radio programs, but in some of their types are the Boundary-Line energy between the physical world and the astral world. In space they have the velocity of light; 186,284 miles per second. At this velocity properties develop which are inconsistent with anything that can be called physical. Yet they are properties too which are inconsistent with the inner-plane or astral world. When velocities exceed that of light, distance, gravitation and time as we know them no longer obtain. But these electromagnetic velocities are in between those of the physical world and those of the inner-plane, and make contact with both. Thus is it that energies of the physical world can only influence the inner-plane world, and the inner-plane world can only contact and influence the physical world, through electromagnetic energies. And while the electromagnetic energies commonly used for this purpose are generated in organic life processes, those which the radio technician uses are similar enough in many of their characteristics that we can learn much relative to the manner in which the two planes of life interact through a study of them. The Boundary-Line energies when they have frequencies that make contact with the inner-plane possible, and the electromagnetic waves which are used in radio, are ruled by Pluto. And as the radio technician must associate with, and understand electromagnetic waves, it is necessary for him to have the thought-cells in his astral body ruled by Pluto active.

These waves, both in the human body and in a radio transmission set, are electrically generated. As Uranus rules electricity, only those with active Uranus thought-cells are strongly enough attracted into association with electrical devices, and have aptitude enough for handling electricity, to become successful radio technicians. There is call also upon active Uranus thought-cells to give the ingenuity and inventive ability for making and handling the various intricate parts involved in radio work.

Where the function of the Uranus thought-cells leaves off and that of the Pluto thought-cells begins, either in radio work or in Intellectual extra-sensory perception, can best be made clear by considering that Uranus rules electricity, and Pluto rules such energy as is radiated by the field that always is present when electricity moves from one point to another. At low frequencies both electricity and its field are dominated almost exclusively by Uranus. The radiation of power into space from an alternating current, for instance, increases as the square of its frequency. The radiation of electromagnetic waves from the ordinary power line, while carrying an alternating current at 60 cycles per second, is negligible due to low frequency. Yet the magnetic field extending some distance from such power lines can be used, through induction, to furnish power. Such a current and its field are almost entirely within the province of Uranus. They have close contact with the low velocity region of the physical world. But what happens when the frequency of the alternating current is stepped up? A kilocycle is 1,000 cycles per second.

In the 60 cycle power line nearly all of the field folds back to be reabsorbed in the conductor. But when the oscillations are many kilocycles, the field does not thus fold back, but continues on into space as the type of waves used in radio. These energies which are thus radiated no longer are under the dominion of Uranus. They acquire properties that make them more akin to the inner-plane than the outer. They pass through the walls of buildings, and reflected from the stratosphere tend to follow round the surface of the earth. Scientists have not decided just what they are, and refer to them as properties of fields in space, or in other vague terms. They are ruled not by Uranus, but by Pluto.

A radio technician, in addition to understanding electricity and how radio waves act, is called upon to build and repair radio apparatus. He thus must have the constructive urge and the mechanical ability which alone are present when there are active Mars thought-cells.

The radio technician also must be alert and intelligent. For these qualities we look chiefly to the Mercury thought-cells. However, a significant percentage of the charts analyzed had Mercury only moderately prominent and the Moon outstanding. It seems that these, instead of depending upon cerebral activity of the Mercury type, were able to make up for it through the use of the faculties of the unconscious mind. That is, with Uranus and Pluto prominent as well as the Moon, they used, probably without knowing it, extra-sensory perception to gain information about the things which it became necessary for them to know. The Moon rules the mentality, and its prominence gives a type of mental activity, even though less devoted to grinding study and cerebral activity than is denoted by a prominent Mercury.

Making and repairing radio sets is not ninth house work. All broadcasting, however, comes under the ninth house. And as the instruments constructed are related either to broadcasting or the reception of that which has been broadcast, there is at least an indirect association with the ninth house. The technician works with apparatus which makes it possible for ninth house activities to take place. Therefore it is well for the radio technician to have an active ninth house.

The Luck Factor—As radio is ruled by Pluto, the aspects which Pluto receives in the birth-chart are the most important factor to consider in determining how lucky an individual will be in radio work. If he is to be also associated with broadcasting in any way, the ninth house, which rules broadcasting, should not be merely active, but its ruler should receive at least one strong harmonious aspect or several weak harmonious aspects.

In broadcasting there is some field for choice of associations. If the efforts are chiefly devoted to broadcasting news, Mercury and the third house should have some harmony. But if the work is chiefly in association with entertainment, the aspects of the ruler of the fifth house become significant. Most radio work at the present day is sponsored by advertisers. The advertiser is ruled by the seventh house, the ruler of which will indicate by its aspects to what extent he will be inclined to be reasonable or even favorable. But the luck in advertising must be determined from the aspects of the ruler of the ninth house.

SALESMAN

Birth-charts of salesmen analyzed	100	100%
Charts with Jupiter or Uranus prominent	100	100%
Charts with Jupiter prominent	92	92%
Charts with Uranus prominent	89	89%
Charts with Mercury prominent	85	85%

In the analysis of the signs in which the Sun, Moon and Ascendant were found in these charts of 100 salesmen, it was found that Leo and Virgo were highest, Aries fewest, with Pisces and Taurus making a poor showing. Yet Aries produced more than one third as many, and Taurus more than one half as many, as the two high signs. Analyzing by Sun sign only, Leo ranked first, with Gemini next. Aries by Sun sign alone produced the fewest, with about one third as many. Yet while Leo seems to be favorable to salesmen, it cannot be considered a birth-chart constant of that vocation. And enough successful salesmen are born under strong influences from all the other signs, and without the more favored signs prominent, that it seems inadvisable to discourage any person from taking up salesmanship merely on the ground that he has Sun, Moon, Ascendant or planets in certain zodiacal signs.

The table, as well as common observation, indicates that there are two distinct types of salesmen. There is the individual who depends upon the good will of his customer to make his sale, and there is the individual who depends upon persuasive powers. Most successful salesmen are to an extent a combination of both types.

The good will type is one who through various acts of friendship, through joviality and perhaps the ability to tell entertaining stories, builds up the impression he is a fine fellow. People patronize him even when they must pay a little more, or go to considerable extra trouble to do so, because they like him so well. On his part, he takes real pleasure in doing favors for people, and will go to no end of trouble to be helpful. In the professions, where the ethics do not permit the individual to advertise as merchants do, nor to boast unduly of his achievements, the individual must depend almost entirely upon his record of past achievement and this good will salesmanship of the friendship, hand-shaking sort, to draw to him patronage and thus sell his abilities. Merchants, however, also find it a great asset. Only those in whose astral bodies the so-called Religious thought-cells are unusually active, such as are mapped by a prominent birth-chart Jupiter, have this type of salesmanship ability.

Glibness of tongue, and a sharp intellect are not to be despised by one who would become a salesman. Ability to express oneself clearly, and to make one's point, have their advantage. But probably cleverness of talk has been over rated as an asset in selling. Such ability is only present in the birth-charts of those who have the Mercury thought-cells unusually active. Yet in only 85% of the salesmen's charts analyzed is Mercury prominent.

The ability to exercise, even though unconsciously, magnetic control over others, however, is very important in salesmanship. High pressure salesmanship of all kinds depends chiefly upon the use of a magnetic personality to beat down sales resistance, and to implant in the prospective customer's mind images of the advantages to be gained through buying, in so forceful a manner that the customer is powerless, temporarily, to resist them.

It is only those having the thought-cells in their unconscious minds mapped by the planet Uranus unusually active who develop within their nervous systems an electrical voltage sufficiently high to be able thus by personal magnetism to sway the minds of others and get them to do their bidding. Such a prominent birth-chart Uranus commonly also gives ability to discern quickly just how the prospect is reacting to the suggestions given him, and to adapt new suggestions based upon these observations. We are warranted, therefore, both from the table and from personal observation of the methods used by salesmen whose charts we have, in concluding that the person who hopes to use the persuasive type of salesmanship successfully, must have a prominent birth-chart Uranus.

Furthermore, the table of analysis reveals that unless either Jupiter or Uranus is prominent in the birth-chart, it is better to discourage such an individual from engaging in salesmanship as his vocation. Those most successful in such work have both Jupiter and Uranus conspicuously prominent in their charts of birth.

The Luck Factor—Salesmanship as a vocation is chiefly under the rule of the financial planet Jupiter. Therefore, the aspects received by Jupiter in the birth-chart have considerable significance in reference to the luck attracted while following this work. However, if Jupiter and Uranus are quite prominent in the birth-chart, too much importance should not be placed upon a badly afflicted Jupiter, as usually it is possible to select something to sell which, because the planet ruling it is well aspected in the birth-chart, will through association attract considerable good luck.

Thus if the Moon were well aspected in the birth-chart, the harmonious activity of the thought-cells thus mapped would tend to bring good luck through selling things the common people need, such as groceries, beverages, and such commodities as can be had at a low price, and selling them in volume to the common people. The five-and-ten stores and their somewhat higher priced offspring are typical environments for Moon salesmanship. Selling to these stores what they retail to the common people is also largely a Moon association in so far as the things sold are concerned, although not in the sense that the merchant to whom the sale was made is under Moon rulership.

If Mercury were well aspected in the birth-chart, the harmonious activity of the thought-cells thus mapped would tend to bring good luck in selling transportation, newspapers, books, study courses, and methods for improving the mind.

If Venus were well aspected in the birth-chart, the harmonious activity of the thought-cells thus mapped would tend to bring good luck through selling jewelry, finery, artistic things, and the articles worn by women. Clothing in general comes under the rulership of Venus; but the less attractive, more serviceable wearing apparels, such as ready-made wear for men, probably has less of the Venus vibration.

If the Sun were well aspected in the birth-chart, the harmonious activity of the thought-cells thus mapped would tend to bring good luck through selling directly to politicians, foremen and executives; selling bonds and gilt edge securities, for instance. The closer the association with those in positions of authority the better.

If Mars were well aspected in the birth-chart, the harmonious activity of the thought-cells thus mapped would tend to bring good luck through selling firearms, ammunition, tools and machinery.

If Jupiter were well aspected in the birth-chart, the harmonious activity of the thought-cells thus mapped would tend to bring good luck through selling the more expensive things which people of wealth alone can buy, or in selling to merchants for purposes of resale.

If Saturn were well aspected in the birth-chart, the harmonious activity of the thought-cells thus mapped would tend to bring good luck through selling real estate, coal, lumber, hay, grain, furniture or insurance. Sales managers must have a prominent birth-chart Saturn.

If Uranus were well aspected in the birth-chart, the harmonious activity of the thought-cells thus mapped would tend to bring good luck through selling automobiles, electrical equipment of all kinds, astrological services, or lately invented ingenious gadgets.

If Neptune were well aspected in the birth-chart, the harmonious activity of the thought-cells thus mapped would tend to bring luck through promoting some enterprise or selling stock, airplanes or air transportation, air conditioning, moving pictures or other entertainment.

If Pluto were well aspected in the birth-chart, the harmonious activity of the thought-cells thus mapped would tend to bring good luck through selling cooperative activities or products, through selling radio or radio equipment, and when they are developed enough to sell to the public, selling television, and power transmitted by wireless.

STENOGRAPHER

Birth-charts of stenographers analyzed	100	100%
Charts with Mercury or Uranus prominent	100	100%
Charts with Uranus aspecting Sun, Moon or Mercury	100	100%
Charts with Mercury prominent	97	97%
Charts with Uranus prominent	97	97%
Charts with Mercury aspecting Uranus	68	68%

Third House Activity of 100 Stenographers

Charts with third house active	98	98%
Charts with planet in third house	51	51%
Charts with third house more discordant than harmonious	59	59%
Charts with third house more harmonious than discordant	40	40%

A tabulation of the 100 charts according to the signs occupied by the Sun, Moon and Ascendant gave Cancer highest, then

Leo, with Virgo a close third. Taurus was lowest and Pisces next lowest, these two signs showing only about half as many as the mentioned high signs. Nevertheless, if the planetary birth-chart constants are shown, there is no valid reason to discourage a person with strong Taurus, or strong Pisces influences from becoming a stenographer.

In all work requiring mental alertness and quick adaptability, as well as in such as is ordinarily considered to be brain work, there should be thought-cells in the astral body of the type mapped by a prominent Mercury. And probably Mercury is prominent in more people's charts than any other planet.

Due to the fact that it is never over 28 degrees along the zodiac from the Sun, and that it revolves around the Sun in a comparatively short period, it is within orb of a conjunction with the Sun frequently. And as both Sun and Mercury move along the zodiac at rather a rapid pace, they make more aspects to the heavier planets than do the more slowly moving orbs. Thus there is opportunity at frequent intervals for people to be born with Mercury fairly prominent in their birth-charts. Not prominent enough to make writers, but prominent enough that if the other constants are present they can become teachers, actors, bookkeepers, waiters, telephone operators or stenographers.

Many stenographers also are competent bookkeepers, and therefore have in their charts the constants of both vocations. Those following both occupations must have Mercury thought-cells active. But those who engage in bookkeeping must have Mars thought-cells active to give them facility with figures, and Saturn thought-cells active to give them plodding care that every little detail is just right. The typical stenographer, who has no bookkeeping inclinations, does not have the patience which monotonous Saturn confers. Instead, he is on his toes with alertness, restless, and whenever possible short-cuts in doing his work.

Not quickness in making calculations, as signified by Mars-Mercury, marks the natural stenographer, but quickness in writing down thought, in grasping the ideas of others, and in making time-saving short-cuts in placing the thoughts of others on paper; ability indicated by active Uranus-Mercury thought-cells.

That which comes into the life through the influence of Uranus nearly always is in some manner due to a human agency. And stenography is work in which there is close contact with some other individual; while a bookkeeper may do most of his work without conversation or close association with another.

Uranus also is the planet of short-cuts. The ability to handle shorthand with facility is typical of Mercury-Uranus thought-cells, as much so as to handle mechanical gadgets is typical activity of the Mars-Uranus thought-cells.

Probably the most favorable single aspect for ability as a stenographer is an aspect between Mercury and Uranus. It will be noticed that 68% of the charts analyzed have this aspect present. Next most favorable seems to be an aspect between Uranus and the Moon, with an aspect between Uranus and the Sun coming third. I believe we are warranted in discouraging anyone from taking up stenography as a vocation in whose chart Uranus, the short-cut planet, is not prominent.

Stenography, quite as much as bookkeeping, requires active third house thought-cells. People who do not have the ruler of the third powerfully aspected, or at least planets in the third, write comparatively little. And a person in whose life little writing is shown is by that indication barred from success as a stenographer.

The Luck Factor—Stenographic work is typically a Mercury occupation; and it is strictly a third house activity. In reference to the luck factors I believe the order of importance is the reverse of that for bookkeepers. While bookkeepers must possess agility in making calculations, it is not the same kind of alertness which is required to take down dictation. A bookkeeper need not consider the time factor in the same way a stenographer does. If he reaches a point where it seems desirable, he can use whatever time is necessary to enable him to handle the matter before him carefully and painstakingly. But a stenographer taking dictation must write down what is said as fast as it is uttered, and is not expected to call upon the one giving dictation often to repeat what was said in the effort to get it down correctly. The speech of the one dictating, and the writing down of what was said by the stenographer, as well as transcribing it, are all typical of Mercury, although the transcribing also is quite as much a third house activity as bookkeeping. I believe, however, that the importance of taking down speech as it is uttered makes Mercury a bit more important in considering the luck factor in the charts of stenographers than the third house.

Yet it is better if the ruler of the third house is well aspected. This would indicate that the individual in association with all manner of third house affairs, including stenographic work, would get so-called lucky breaks. On the other hand, if there were no good aspects to the ruler of the third, and powerfully discordant ones were present, the stenographer, in following an occupation for which there might be unusual talent, would attract many so-called unlucky breaks.

Yet we must not jump to the conclusion that just because there are heavily afflicted planets in the third, or the ruler of the third, or Mercury, is heavily afflicted that the individual should be discouraged from taking up stenography. Even discordant aspects indicate natural aptitude, and unless there is no help from harmonious aspects, such natural aptitude may be ample to overcome the so-called unlucky breaks encountered. Most stenographers' charts have both discordant and harmonious aspects to Mercury, and both discordant and harmonious aspects to the ruler of the third house.

Uranus represents largely a human influence. Afflictions to Uranus thus commonly indicate misfortunes brought about through contact with others. And if Mercury, chief ruler of stenography, is afflicted by Uranus, the association with stenography as a vocation tends to attract the individual to a human association where the affliction can work out. One may also say that a discordant aspect between Uranus and the Sun tends to cause affliction through the boss or one in authority, and that a discordant aspect between Uranus and the Moon tends to cause affliction through the influence of women or common people. A harmonious aspect between Mercury, the ruler of stenography, and Uranus, not only gives ability, but is a decided luck attracting aspect for those following this vocation.

STORE CLERK

Birth-charts of store clerks analyzed... 100   100%
Charts with Saturn prominent... 100   100%
Charts with Pluto prominent... 99   99%
Charts with Jupiter prominent... 98   98%
Charts with Moon prominent... 97   97%
Charts with Mercury prominent... 96   96%

First House Activity of 100 Store Clerks
Charts with first house active... 95   95%
Charts with planet in first house... 62   62%
Charts with first house more discordant than harmonious 50   50%
Charts with first house more harmonious than discordant. 50   50%

Seventh House Activity of 100 Store Clerks
Charts with seventh house active... 94   94%
Charts with planet in seventh house... 51   51%
Charts with seventh house more discordant than harmonious 51   51%
Charts with seventh house more harmonious than discordant 49   49%

A tabulation of the 100 charts according to signs occupied by the Sun, Moon and Ascendant gave Libra highest, then Leo, with Pisces third. Taurus and Cancer were lowest with a little more than two-thirds the number to be found in Libra. Next lowest were Aries, Gemini, Virgo and Aquarius; each of these containing the same number.

The more common motive which prompts an individual to go into business is the desire for economic safety. People who fear a time may arrive when they will be in want for food, clothing and shelter, or when they will be in want for less essential material things which they desire to possess, are impelled to strive to prevent such an occurence. And one of the most common ways of preventing such want and the suffering it brings is to trade with others who have what is desired, or with others who have the medium of exchange that will enable that which is desired to be purchased. The bargainer, the shrewd trader, the individual who takes to business because he likes it, has the thought-cells mapped by a prominent Saturn in his birth-chart. And while store clerks need not be good bargainers, to feel at home in the atmosphere of trade, and to follow day after day, the required routine, they should have a prominent Saturn in their charts of birth.

Jupiter is the salesmanship planet. He thrives not on bargains, but on the good will of others. To the extent Jupiter is a dominant influence in the life will people go out of their way to do the individual favors. And to be a successful store clerk the individual should thus be able, in some measure, to attract patronage. People will walk blocks farther, and right past a store where they can buy to greater advantage where a typically Saturn individual is behind the counter, in order to make purchases of a clerk whose Jupiter is prominent enough to give him genial warmth and an atmosphere of joviality. To be sure, a store clerk need not have the salesmanship ability that is requisite in some lines. It is not even necessary that he have the high-pressure magnetism conferred by a prominent Uranus. But he should have some measure of the salesmanship qualities which are denoted in a birth-chart only when Jupiter is prominent in it.

A store clerk need not be a student, need not have wide information; but he should be able to talk with some measure of intelligence to his customers. Customers like to have some interest shown in their affairs and problems. There are certain bits of information which they are pleased to receive. And the clerk should be able to explain the points of the goods he endeavors to sell. Also there is the matter of making out a bill for whatever goods are sold, and keeping the record of sales straight; all of which makes certain demands upon the Mercury type of intelligence. It is an advantage therefore, for a store clerk to have Mercury prominent in his chart of birth.

The people in general, as distinct from any particular class, are ruled by the Moon. If an individual is to attract into his life constant contacts with large numbers of people he should thus have the Moon prominent in his chart of birth. Not only are the common people, which most store clerks daily contact, ruled by the Moon, but this luminary also rules women; and in America, at least, women do the majority of the store buying. A prominent Moon in the birth-chart makes it that much easier for women to take an important place in the life. Whether they will affect it harmoniously or discordantly, of course, must be determined by its aspects.

But it was found in the analysis of 100 charts that Pluto was prominent even more often than Jupiter, Mercury or the Moon. Pluto has to do with mobs of people and with people in groups, and it relates to co-operative ability. There are stores, no doubt, where people come only singly or in pairs; but in most stores there are special occasions, such as sales, when groups of people must be handled; and a prominent Pluto seems to aid in this. Likewise there are stores where a clerk is quite independent of others. But usually a clerk, to be successful in his vocation, must possess the ability to co-operate with the boss at least, and more often than not with a number of other clerks. For an organization to function effectively, whether it be in a store or a political movement, there must be an attitude of all working for a single objective. A certain amount of loyalty to the organization is demanded, and the ability to overlook friction and personal bias in a co-operative effort to further the interests of all. Such ability is conferred by active thought-cells such as are mapped by Pluto.

The success of a store clerk depends upon the impression he creates with the public he is compelled to contact daily. This impression is indicated not merely by Saturn and Jupiter, but also by his own personality, indicated by the first house, and by the personalities of the public he attracts, indicated by the seventh house. He needs active first house thought-cells to give him personality and personal activity, and he needs active seventh house thought-cells to attract to him, for good or ill, the public. People who do not have active seventh house thought-cells do not have constant contacts with the public.

The Luck Factor—Of first importance in reference to the luck factor are the aspects received by the planet, or planets, ruling the seventh house. If the seventh house is shown to be quite discordant, constant difficulties will arise in dealing with the public; but if the seventh house is active, and its ruler well aspected, there will be important contacts with the public, and they will prove harmonious and of advantage. However, many store clerks succeed in holding their jobs in spite of considerable difficulty with customers.

Clerking in a store is ruled chiefly by Saturn. Usually, however, there are rulers relating to what is handled which are even more important to consider from the luck standpoint. A hardware clerk thus has more association with Mars, a clothing clerk with Venus, a radio clerk with Pluto, and an electrical appliance clerk with Uranus. Thus, after considering the seventh house, the luck factor should be considered from the type of merchandise which chiefly is sold.

TEACHER

Birth-charts of teachers analyzed	100	100%
Charts with Mercury prominent	84	84%

Ninth House Activity of 100 Teachers

Charts with ninth house active	96	96%
Charts with planet in ninth house	51	51%
Charts with ninth house more discordant than harmonious	61	61%
Charts with ninth house more harmonious than discordant	38	38%

Fifth House Activity of 100 Teachers

Charts with fifth house active	92	92%
Charts with planet in fifth house	45	45%
Charts with fifth house more discordant than harmonious	60	60%
Charts with fifth house more harmonious than discordant	39	39%

An analysis of the signs in which the Sun, Moon and Ascendant of each of these 100 charts is found does not indicate that any of the signs can be considered birth-chart constants of teaching. The Sun, Moon or Ascendant in Gemini, Virgo or Sagittarius, however, seems to attract to teaching as a profession more often than other signs do. Also, every additional aspect to Mercury seems to give aid in this direction.

Mercury is the planet mapping the thought-cells within the unconscious mind which have most direct association with the electrical currents which flow over the nerves, and which are responsible for objective thinking. Thinking in terms of words and sentences is a type of conscious activity dependent upon the use of the electromagnetic energies ruled by Mercury; to convey that which the unconscious mind desires to express, to the physical cells of the brain. That is, the activity of the brain cells is dependent upon the activity of the thought-cells which Mercury maps in the birth-chart. Thus it is common to speak of Mercury as the planet of mental expression.

Those who express themselves through writing or speech, to be successful, must have the Intellectual thought-cells more than commonly active; which means that Mercury must be prominent in the birth-chart. And the study of the charts of 100 teachers reveals that to the extent Mercury is thus prominent and strongly aspected is there ability to impart information to others. Each aspect of Mercury, connecting it by a stellar aerial with another distinct group of thought-cells, gives ability to impart information of a different kind. Thus the more numerous the aspects which Mercury makes, the greater is the facility to grasp and teach a variety of subjects.

Uranus, also closely associated with the nerve currents, gives a similar ability in imparting information. But because it so strongly is attracted to things new or uncommon, its prominence is not noticeable among teachers in the public schools. Among those who teach astrology and occultism it is nearly always prominent.

Those who teach, advertise, publish, lecture, or otherwise give public expression to their opinions, also are exercising the thought-cells mapped in their astral bodies by the ninth house. Any planet in the ninth house, and to a less pronounced degree, the ruler of the cusp of the ninth house, influences somewhat the manner in which the opinions are thus publicly expressed.

The Luck Factor—The luck factor in the vocation of teaching is to some extent indicated by the aspects made by the planet Mercury, which is general ruler of this profession. And it is also signified by the aspects made to the ruler of the ninth house.

In teaching, as in writing, it often is possible to select the subject taught. If the planet Mars were afflicted by Mercury and the ruler of the ninth house, strife and difficulties would be attracted in the attempt to teach mathematics or mechanical training. But if at the same time, either Mercury or the ruler of the ninth were in good aspect to Uranus, much luck might be expected from teaching astrology or electrical engineering.

Or if Mercury has any aspect to a planet, and that planet is otherwise well aspected, much luck could be expected from teaching a subject ruled by the planet. That is, if the person has ability to teach a subject, which usually requires that Mercury makes some aspect to the planet ruling it, the more harmonious in the chart the planet is which rules the subject the more luck would be attracted in teaching it, or otherwise associating with it.

Of those who are teachers of children, and of those who are teachers of music, the analysis shows that they almost invariably have an unusually active fifth house. The luck in thus associating with children or music, of course, is indicated by the aspects made to the ruler of the fifth.

Among those who are teachers of astrology, occultism or metaphysics, the power of the aspects to the ruler of the fifth was not noticeable. In such teaching, and in lecture work in general, the thought-cells mapped by the ninth house must be active to give the type of energy which draws the person into thus expressing himself publicly. But the public thus addressed is chiefly represented by the seventh house. Therefore to discern the reaction of the public thus addressed, and the luck factor in relation to it, the aspects of the ruler of the seventh house should be considered.

In teaching, as in most work where the hazard is not outstanding, it is probable that ability, as indicated by a prominent Mercury and an active ninth house, is able to overcome a large amount of birth-chart discord. Even with one harmonious aspect to Mercury or to the ruler of the ninth, it would not be advisable to discourage an individual from taking up teaching, provided the thought-cells mapped by Mercury and the ninth house were active enough.

On the other hand, no matter if such aspects as Mercury and the ruler of the ninth house had were all harmonious; unless Mercury were prominent, and the ruler of the ninth was powerfully aspected, it would be well to discourage teaching as a vocation.

TELEPHONE OPERATOR

Birth-charts of telephone operators analyzed	100	100%
Charts with Mercury prominent	98	98%
Charts with Uranus prominent	98	98%
Charts with Pluto prominent	96	96%
Charts with Moon prominent	95	95%

Third House Activity of 100 Telephone Operators

Charts with third house active	100	100%
Charts with planet in third house	65	65%
Charts with third house more discordant than harmonious	61	61%
Charts with third house more harmonious than discordant	39	39%

A tabulation of the 100 charts according to the signs occupied by the Sun, Moon and Ascendant gave some variation according to signs, but nothing outstanding enough to be considered a birth-chart constant, or markedly to encourage or discourage taking up telephone work.

Whatever the occupation may be, if it requires alertness and quick responsiveness, to be successful in it necessitates that Mercury be prominent in the birth-chart.

The prominence of Uranus in the charts of telephone operators probably has little connection with the magnetic power to influence the minds of others given by this planet. Instead, it is likely it relates to the association with something electrical, such as Uranus rules, and with the various gadgets which are an essential part of a telephone system.

Pluto, on the other hand, rules groups of people, such as a telephone operator serves. It is noticeable that those who contact groups of people, either working with them, or serving them, have this upper-octave of the Moon prominent in their charts of birth.

The significance of the Moon is quite obvious, although it is less often prominent than Mercury, Uranus or Pluto. The Moon rules the common people. And it is the common people, as a rule, who keep a telephone operator busy. It is true that there are calls from all classes, but even so, the Moon must be taken as the general ruler of the people; and much of the conversation which is carried on over a telephone is distinctly of the Moon type, gossipy and commonplace, about domestic affairs and trifles, rather than on the intellectual or informative plane of Mercury.

The Luck Factor—The associations of a telephone operator in her work are chiefly the electrical appliances ruled by Uranus, and the calls that are ruled by the third house. Every harmonious aspect Uranus receives, therefore, assists in attracting luck through contacts made with the switchboard, and through the electrical system which is essential to her work.

But probably of still more importance as influencing the luck factor is the third house. The third house rules the calls that are made, and the conversation which takes place by means of the telephone system. And as it is the avenue through which the operator is brought into contact with those she serves, and often the only avenue of contact between herself and those placing calls, to a great extent it determines whether or not her services are satisafctory, and the general attitude toward her of those she contacts over the wire. And as contacts over the telephone, or in association with it, sometimes lead to acquaintanceships of a more personal nature, which may benefit or injure socially or financially, this third house influence may lead to conditions that make or mar the life.

This does not signify that a person should refuse to take up telephone work merely because Uranus or the third house is badly afflicted, as the analysis shows that 61% of such operators have an afflicted third house. But it does mean that at least one strong harmonious aspect to Uranus or the ruler of the third house is an advantage, and that the more harmonious the third house and Uranus are, if they are quite powerful, the more luck will be attracted in this vocation.

WAITER

Birth-charts of waiters or waitresses analyzed	100	100%
Charts with Mars prominent	99	99%
Charts with Moon prominent	96	96%
Charts with Neptune prominent	96	96%
Charts with Pluto prominent	96	96%
Charts with Mercury prominent	91	91%

Sixth House Activity of 100 Waiters

Charts with sixth house active	95	95%
Charts with planet in sixth house	48	48%
Charts with sixth house more discordant than harmonious	40	40%
Charts with sixth house more harmonious than discordant	60	60%
Charts with ruler of sixth actually in tenth or in close aspect to ruler of tenth	72	72%

First House Activity of 100 Waiters

Charts with first house active	94	94%
Charts with planet in first house	62	62%
Charts with first house more discordant than harmonious	42	42%
Charts with first house more harmonious than discordant	57	57%
Charts with first house outstanding in attractive, affable, magnetic and pleasing personality	88	88%

An analysis of the signs in which the Sun, Moon and Ascendant of these 100 charts are found does not indicate any of the signs can be considered birth-chart constants of waiters. Sun, Moon or Ascendant in Gemini, Leo or Sagittarius seems to attract the individual to this calling more often than the other signs do, however, and Aquarius, Taurus or Aries least often. The three high signs mentioned contain about twice as many waiters as the three mentioned low signs.

The prominence of Mars in the chart of a waiter seems to be necessary to give the muscular strength for the amount of walking required, and to carry trays of food.

The Moon is the planet of the people to be served, and relates to nutrition and to the foods and beverages with which a waiter is constantly associated in his work. It seems that when the thought-cells it maps in the unconscious mind are unusually active, this facilitates work in which foods are handled.

The social urges ruled by Venus seem to express on a higher plane through the thought-cells ruled by Neptune. These social urges express as friendliness. But the kind of friendliness best suited to a waiter is not of the Venus kind, but one which is entirely related to his art of serving. That is, while Venus is distinctly personal, Neptune is able to attain the broader impersonal, yet courteous and friendly attitude which a good waiter displays. Neptune is natural ruler of the house of restrictions (twelfth), and while a waiter should be friendly, in that friendly spirit of accommodation he is not supposed to overstep very rigid restrictions. He is supposed to enter into conversation only when asked some question, and at other times to be as unobtrusive as possible.

The prominence of Pluto in a waiter's chart is readily understood when it is recalled that Pluto attracts to groups, and more often than not a waiter does not serve a single individual at a time, but a party of individuals. Most people when they dine, like to dine in the company of others. And it is customary to serve the whole party the same course of the meal at one time.

As Pluto and the Moon seem to be octaves of each other, it should be noted also that when one of these orbs is not prominent in the chart of a waiter the other one is.

Mercury is the natural ruler of the house of foods (sixth), but probably of greater importance in giving natural ability as a waiter is its influence over manual dexterity, alertness and a good temporary memory. Waiters often are required to juggle dishes and trays in a manner quite disconcerting to the sluggish. And often they are required to remember a long list of items, or special requirements, of their customers. Active Mercury thought-cells give facility in these matters.

While the sixth house maps the thought-cells relating to the conditions surrounding all kinds of work; those constantly at the beck and call of others, as are waiters, seem to require that these thought-cells be unusually energetic. To be energetic, it is not necessary that they be mapped by a planet in the sixth house. But the ruler of the sixth must receive powerful aspects.

Success as a waiter depends not merely upon muscular strength, agility and ability to remember the customer's wants, but also in rather marked degree upon an attractive and affable personality. Perhaps the continuous moving about which is part of a waiter's work in some degree makes it necessary that the first house thought-cells should be active, as mapped by the ruler of the first receiving powerful aspects. But in addition to this, the analysis of the 100 charts reveals that a great majority of them have a first house which denotes a pleasing personality. It seems, therefore, that a first house indicating both activity and affability are assets to those following this vocation.

The Luck Factor—As the occupation is so closely associated both with all types of people and with nutrition, the Moon, which rules both, is a luck factor to be considered. That is, one who has thought-cells which are mapped by a well aspected Moon tends to attract good fortune in association with crowds of people and with dining.

And as the occupation relates to the sixth house, the house both of foods and of serving, the aspects to the ruler of the sixth should be taken into consideration in determining the luck, or absence of it, while engaged in this type of work.

It is not essential that the ruler of the first house be entirely harmonious. The more harmonious aspects the ruler of the first has, and the fewer discordant ones, the less friction is apt to arise with those served. But it seems better to have a powerful, even though quite heavily afflicted first house, than to have one weak but free from discords.

While an afflicted Moon, an afflicted first house and an afflicted sixth house, are no bars to a moderate amount of success as a waiter, it will be far easier to create a demand for such service if the Moon, the ruler of the first house, and the ruler of the sixth house, each receives at least one moderately powerful harmonious aspect, such as a sextile or a trine. And the more powerful these planets are, and the more harmonious the aspects they receive, the more luck can be expected while following the vocation of waiter.

WRITER

Birth-charts of writers analyzed	100	100%
Charts with Mercury prominent	95	95%
Charts with Mercury aspecting Moon or Sun	91	91%
Charts with Mercury aspecting Moon	64	64%
Charts with Mercury conjunction Sun	58	58%

Third House Activity of 100 Writers

Charts with third house active	97	97%
Charts with planet in third house	49	49%
Charts with third house more discordant than harmonious	58	58%
Charts with third house more harmonious than discordant	40	40%

Ninth House Activity of 100 Writers

Charts with ninth house active	94	94%
Charts with planet in ninth house	46	46%
Charts with ninth house more discordant than harmonious	51	51%
Charts with ninth house more harmonious than discordant	49	49%

A tabulation of the signs in which the Sun, Moon and Ascendant were located in the charts of these 100 writers revealed no sign which stood out with sufficient prominence to warrant special mention, and certainly no sign can be considered a birthchart constant of writers.

The thought-cells mapped by Mercury are those which give facility in expressing the thoughts through written or spoken language. With certain notable exceptions, the extent of their activity is a measure of the ability to write. Sometimes an unusually prominent Uranus, as in the charts of Charles Dickens and Herbert Spencer; or an unusually prominent Moon, in the case of those who write largely through impressions they get psychically; acts successfully as a substitute for a prominent Mercury. The five charts tabulated, in which Mercury was not prominent, were those of writers of outstanding recognition.

First of all, however, one who aspires to write, should have exceptional knowledge of some kind. Many people know much about some special subject, but because the Mercury thought-cells are not active enough, they cannot impart that knowledge to others in writing. Thus the prominence of the writer commonly is measured, not by the prominence of Mercury, but by the power and ability shown in the chart as a whole; Mercury merely indicating ability successfully to express what is known in print.

I believe what is here meant can best be driven home by a study of the birth-charts of writers. O. O. McIntyre is said to have been the highest paid journalist in the world. He had the Moon in the house of newspapers (third) and three planets in the house of publishing (ninth).

But there are a wide variety of writers who never were journalists. They write about that of which they have special knowledge. George Bernard Shaw, with Neptune the most elevated planet, in close trine to Mercury, is best known for his plays. Conan Doyle, with most of his planets in the house of secret things (twelfth), is best known for his Sherlock Holmes stories and his writings about spiritualism. Upton Sinclair, with socialistic (Neptune) and universal welfare (Pluto) planets conjunction his M.C., is best known for his socialistic books.

In writing, as in other arts, dramatic expression, in great measure, depends upon the activity of the thought-cells mapped by Neptune. And in addition to its prominence, the writing of fiction is facilitated by the prominence of the Moon, which also gives vividness to the imagination. Jack London had Mercury opposition Moon and square Neptune; while Bulwer-Lytton had Moon conjunction Ascendant and trine Neptune.

Writing is an activity associated with the third house, and only those with active third house thought-cells are apt to be attracted to this association strongly enough to make it as important as it must be in one who does much writing.

But for success as a writer who gets his material published over his own name, there must also be active ninth house thought-cells. A copy-writer in a newspaper office, or a reporter for a newspaper whose name does not appear in association with what he writes, keeps within the province of the third house, and does not need much ninth house activity. Perhaps the so-called ghost writers, who write articles, biographies and other material for prominent people whose names appear as the authors, do not need active ninth house thought-cells. The ninth house thought-cells, however, must be active if the individual is to receive recognition for what he writes. Thus a journalist who aspires to get his material published over his by-line needs active ninth house thought-cells.

The Luck Factor—The luck in getting material published, except newspaper copy for which no credit is given and which is rewritten before publication, primarily is indicated by the aspects of the ninth house. People who have active ninth house thought-cells, even though there is no harmonious aspect to the ruler of the ninth, get material published; but have great obstacles to overcome in so doing. It is much better for a writer to have at least one powerful harmonious aspect to the ruler of the ninth or several weak harmonious aspects. The luck attracted in reference to the public expression of ideas through publications, speech or radio, is chiefly indicated by the harmony or discord of the ninth house thought-cells.

The luck in association with newspapers is indicated by the aspects of the third house. Mercury is the general ruler of writing and printing. Its aspects, therefore, have secondary significance in reference to the luck attracted in getting material published and in reference to what is brought into the life through such writings as are published.

Printed in the United Kingdom
by Lightning Source UK Ltd.
109112UKS00002B/329